θωκ 3/04

England and Europe

1485–1603

SEMINAR STUDIES IN HISTORY

General Editor: Roger Lockyer

England and Europe
1485–1603

Susan Doran

LONGMAN
London and New York

LONGMAN GROUP UK LIMITED
Longman House, Burnt Mill, Harlow, Essex CM20 2JE, England
and Associated Companies throughout the world

Published in the United States of America
by Longman Inc., New York

First published 1986
Fifth impression 1992
ISBN 0 582 35412 9

Set in 10/11 pt Linotron Baskerville
Printed in Malaysia by VP

The Publisher's policy is to use paper manufactured from sustainable forests.

British Library Cataloguing in Publication Data

Doran, Susan
England and Europe, 1485–1603. – (Seminar
studies in history)
1. Europe – Foreign relations – Great Britain
2. Great Britain – Foreign relations – Europe
3. Great Britain – Foreign relations – 1485–1603
I. Title   II. Series
327.4042   D34.G7

ISBN 0–582–35412–9

Library of Congress Cataloging in Publication Data

Doran, Susan.
England and Europe, 1485–1603.
(Seminar studies in history)
Bibliography: p.
Includes index.
1. Great Britain – Foreign relations – 1485–1603.
2. Great Britain – Foreign relations – Europe. 3. Europe – Foreign
relations – Great Britain. I. Title II. Series.
DA315.D67   1986   327.4104   85–19698
ISBN 0–582–35412–9

Contents

INTRODUCTION TO THE SERIES   vii
PREFACE   ix

Part One: The Background   1
1 INTERNATIONAL CONTEXT   1

2 OVERSEAS TRADE   4

3 MILITARY RESOURCES   7

4 THE MAKING OF FOREIGN POLICY   12

Part Two: Analysis   15
5 HENRY VII 1485–1509   15
  Introduction   15
  Policy of peace   15
  Threats to the dynasty   17
  The last years   20
  Conclusion   22

6 HENRY VIII   23
  1509–14   23
  Wolsey   25
  1515–26   27
  1527–40   32

7 MID-TUDOR ENGLAND 1540–63   38
  Introduction   38
  1540–47   39
  Edward VI 1547–53   46
  Mary 1553–58   50
  Elizabeth I 1558–63   55

Contents

8 ELIZABETH I 1564–1603   60
   Spain 1564–85   60
   France 1564–85   70
   War 1585–1603   76

   Part Three: Assessment   81

   Part Four: Documents   84

   BIBLIOGRAPHY   107
   GLOSSARY   114
   INDEX   115

Maps

Southern Scotland and the Border   42
Northern France and the Netherlands   65

Seminar Studies in History
Founding Editor: Patrick Richardson

Introduction

The Seminar Studies series was conceived by Patrick Richardson, whose experience of teaching history persuaded him of the need for something more substantial than a textbook chapter but less formidable than the specialised full-length academic work. He was also convinced that such studies, although limited in length, should provide an up-to-date and authoritative introduction to the topic under discussion as well as a selection of relevant documents and a comprehensive bibliography.

Patrick Richardson died in 1979, but by that time the Seminar Studies series was firmly established, and it continues to fulfil the role he intended for it. This book, like others in the series, is therefore a living tribute to a gifted and original teacher.

Note on the System of References:
A bold number in round brackets (**5**) in the text refers the reader to the corresponding entry in the Bibliography section. A bold number in square brackets, preceded by 'doc.' [**doc. 6**], refers the reader to the corresponding item in the section of Documents, which follows the main text. An asterisk (*) after a word or phrase refers the reader to the corresponding entry in the Glossary, which follows the Bibliography at the end of the book.

ROGER LOCKYER
General Editor

Acknowledgements

We are grateful to the following for permission to reproduce copyright material:

The Bodley Head for an extract from *The Fugger News Letters* by V. Von Klarmill (trans. L. S. R. Byrne); the Controller of Her Majesty's Stationery Office for an extract from *List and Analysis of State Papers*, Foreign Series, Elizabeth I, Vol. III ed. R. B. Wernham; Macmillan Publishing Co. for an extract from pp. 36–7 of *The Letters of Henry VIII* ed. M. St Clare Byrne, originally published by Cassell & Co. Ltd © 1936; Public Record Office for an extract from State Papers SP12/35/38.

We are grateful to the following for permission to adapt maps:

Cambridge University Press for map adapted from W. E. Wilkie *The Cardinal Protectors of England, Rome and the Tudors before the Reformation*, 1974; Jonathan Cape for map slightly adapted from R. B. Wernham, *Before the Armada: The Growth of English Foreign Policy 1485–1588*, 1966.

Cover: detail of Jean de Dinteville and Georges de Selve ('The Ambassadors') by Hans Holbein the Younger, 1533. Reproduced by courtesy of the Trustees, The National Gallery, London.

Preface

I would like to acknowledge my great debt to the late Prof. Joel Hurstfield whose encouragement was crucial to my development as a historian. Thanks are also due to many of my past students for asking the right questions and to my husband for doing the practical tasks which writers usually seem to leave to their wives: typing, proof-reading and editing.

Finally, I want to thank Roger Lockyer for suggesting the book in the first place and for carefully reading and correcting the first draft.

Part One: The Background

1 International Context

For most of the Tudor period Spain and France dominated the European arena, and the rivalry between them was a central feature of international politics. Both states by the 1490s had emerged as strong and powerful after a long period of internal disunity, weak government and partial occupation by foreign powers. In 1479 the Crowns of Aragon and Castile were united in the persons of Ferdinand and Isabella. They reconquered Granada in the south from the Moors in 1492, the same year that Columbus, under their patronage, began the voyage which was to bring Spain an overseas empire. The Spanish monarchs strengthened their position *vis-à-vis* the Spanish nobles, the church and the towns, whilst creating a centralised authority in their kingdoms, especially Castile. In France a succession of able rulers from Charles VII onwards reasserted royal power and regained lands once conquered or alienated from the Crown. All the territories held by England, save Calais, had been restored to Charles VII by 1453. Picardy, the Somme towns and the ancestral duchy of Burgundy were returned to Louis XI after a series of clashes with his arch-enemy Charles, Duke of Burgundy. The duchy of Brittany was annexed by Charles VII in 1492. The French kings eroded the privileges of nobles, *pays* and *parlement*, whilst gaining the effective right of taxing at will.

The focal point of rivalry between these two powers from 1494 to 1559 was Italy. The conflict had small beginnings: the rival dynastic claims of Anjou (Charles VIII) and Aragon to the insignificant and impoverished kingdom of Naples. There were also minor disputes over Cerdagne, Roussillon, Perpignan and Navarre on the Franco-Spanish border. French ambitions in Italy were extended to Milan in 1499 after the accession of Louis XII who had a personal claim to that duchy. The ensuing Italian Wars (1494–1515) ended with the Spanish conquest of Naples and the French capture and then loss of Milan.

A new dimension to Franco-Spanish rivalry arose around the person of Charles V. As Duke of Burgundy (1506), King of Spain

(1510), ruler of Austrian Habsburg lands (1518) and Holy Roman Emperor (1519), he impinged on the interests and security of France. First, he ruled over lands which were nominally French fiefs (Artois and Flanders) and which had been coveted by the French King since the reign of Louis XI. Then, he inherited the disputes over Naples and the territories along the Pyrenees. Furthermore, Milan was an Imperial fief * and more importantly the vital bridge from Charles's territories in the Netherlands, Germany and Franche-Comté to Naples. Finally, France was virtually encircled by Habsburg lands; her borders were vulnerable to Spanish troops (Artois and Flanders were but 290 kilometres from Paris) whilst any move to expand eastwards would be blocked by a strong hostile power. Dynastic and strategic considerations thus combined to create an intense Habsburg–Valois rivalry to be fought out in a series of wars from 1515 to 1559.

Exhaustion of resources, not the cessation of differences, brought about the end of the wars in the 1559 Treaty of Câteau-Cambrésis. Consequently, Franco-Spanish hostility continued, but as a latent feature of the second half of the sixteenth century. It was latent, not open, because of the French civil wars (1562–98). The collapse of the French monarchy's power in the face of doctrinal strife and aristocratic rebellion prevented France from renewing the wars or even from exploiting effectively Spain's own weaknesses; for Spain too had major problems. The Netherlands were in rebellion in 1566 and again from 1572. At times, the French tried to aid the rebels for their own ends – Coligny in 1571 and Alençon from 1576 till his death in 1584 – but their help was mainly ineffectual. It was Philip II of Spain who broke the uneasy peace when he ordered Parma, commander of the Flanders army, to invade France in 1590 to prevent the Huguenot,* Henry of Navarre, from becoming King. Fear of further and greater French aid to the Dutch rebels, as well as religious considerations, prompted his actions. The war which followed marked the recovery of France, as hatred of Spain over-rode domestic doctrinal differences. The Treaty of Vervins (1598) ended the war but again not permanently. Franco-Spanish rivalry was to dominate the seventeenth century as it had the sixteenth century.

This was the context within which English foreign policy had to operate. Franco-Spanish hostility brought some security to England, as did the internal problems of the two states after 1560.

*Asterisked words are explained in the Glossary on page 114.

As the Earl of Sussex expressed it in 1577: 'the troubles of both places when they have been carried jointly have certainly bred our quiet, and so would continue it if they jointly are continued' (**119**, p. 346). Yet English governments, without the benefit of hindsight, did not know when a peace might be made permanently or internal problems be settled. French support for a pretender, French intrigues in Scotland, French ambitions in Flanders and a Catholic crusade initiated by either France or Spain were spectres to haunt English governments during the Tudor period. Franco-Spanish rivalry also provided some opportunities for England. If she chose to embark on campaigns to win back her French territories, she could be assured of a powerful ally.

2 Overseas Trade

In the first half of the sixteenth century, the primary export of England was undyed woollen cloth. Most of it was destined for Antwerp where it was exchanged for a variety of foreign goods. The Antwerp money market with its banking, credit and insurance facilities was also widely used by Englishmen, and came to be the main source of government loans from 1544 to 1574. The English economy was so dependent on Antwerp that a foreign observer could cynically remark: 'If Englishmen's fathers were hanged in Antwerp's gate, their children would creep betwixt their legs to come into the said town' (**71**, p. 9).

This fundamental economic fact had repercussions on English foreign policy. First, the government of both England and the Netherlands recognised the importance of the London–Antwerp trade axis and were consequently anxious to keep on good terms with each other. Secondly, both were prepared to use the trade as a political bargaining counter. Thirdly, England's attempts to escape her dependence on the Antwerp market resulted in diplomatic overtures towards other states, and government backing for traders, explorers, even privateers seeking new markets.

Economic considerations combined with political interests in encouraging English rulers to maintain friendly relations with the rulers of the Netherlands during the first three-quarters of the Tudor period. Yet whenever serious political differences arose between the two governments, each would sacrifice, or rather use as a weapon, economic interests to obtain political advantages. Thus, in retaliation for Burgundian support for the pretender, Perkin Warbeck, Henry VII imposed a trade embargo on the Netherlands and ordered the Merchant Adventurers to move from Antwerp to Calais. The Netherlands' government responded in kind, but was the first to give way, in 1496, though probably for political reasons rather than because of economic pressure. Henry VIII tried unsuccessfully to employ similar tactics in the 1520s against Charles V. In 1563–4 and 1568–74, the Netherlands' government placed an embargo on English trade as a retaliation against English aid to protestants abroad, and more specifically in 1568 against Elizabeth's seizure of Spanish treasure ships. These economic sanctions, even though not totally effective, harmed England more than the Netherlands and revealed her vulnerability in being so heavily reliant on one outlet for her goods [**doc. 1**].

There were also sound economic reasons for the government to try to reduce England's dependence on the Antwerp market and find new outlets elsewhere. Henry VII appreciated this point. Not only did he work to strengthen England's trading position in the Netherlands by negotiating the *Intercursus Magnus* (1496) and *Intercursus Malus* (1506); at the same time he used diplomacy to diversify into other markets and his patronage to encourage the discovery of new trade routes. In 1489 and 1490 he negotiated with Denmark an agreement aimed at extending English trade in the Baltic. The 1378 commercial treaty with Portugal was renewed in 1489; a new Anglo-French commercial treaty was signed in 1497. There were also a treaty with Florence (1490), commercial clauses in treaties with Spain (1489 and 1499) and an abortive treaty with Riga (1499). Henry became patron of first John Cabot and then his son, Sebastian, in their search for new lands (**22**). In effect, Henry's efforts paid low dividends; comparatively few English traders forsook the security of the Antwerp market for more risky ventures elsewhere and the royal initiative was not continued under his son. It was the 1550 collapse of the Antwerp cloth market, due to over-production, that forced traders once again to seek new routes and markets further afield. They found government backing. Northumberland was the patron of the French pilot Jean Ribault, Sebastian Cabot and John Dee; and he encouraged the search for the northeast and north-west passages. The government promoted attempts to open trade with Morocco, the Gold Coast and China, and negotiated a trade treaty with Sweden. Mary's government assisted in the formation of the Muscovy Company, although Mary herself had little interest in encouraging English trade – no doubt because of the potential conflict with Spain. Indeed her husband, Philip II, in response to Portuguese complaints about the English traders breaking into their monopoly in Guinea, ordered the Spanish ambassador in England to stop a proposed English voyage to the Portuguese islands [**doc. 2a**]. A more decisive impulse was provided for this movement towards developing new markets after 1564 when the political disturbances in the Netherlands disrupted the Antwerp market and necessitated the finding of alternative outlets. Emden was used temporarily as a cloth staple* during the

1564 crisis; Hamburg made an agreement with the Merchant Adventurers in 1567 which allowed the town to be an English cloth staple for ten years. By the end of the century, Middelburg, Emden, Stade and Hamburg were the main outlets for English cloth. The government consulted with the merchants in the choice of these towns and gave the trade its support whenever it could. Elizabeth gave diplomatic support to trade in less conventional regions as well; some diplomatic concessions were granted to the Czar and the Sultan in return for substantial economic privileges for the newly formed trading companies in Russia and the Levant. Elizabeth defended the maritime activities of Hawkins, Drake, Gilbert, Frobisher and Raleigh when they provoked howls of protest from the Portuguese and Spaniards (**71, 90**).

By the end of the Tudor period the pattern of overseas trade had changed. 'New markets had been found, new companies incorporated to exploit them, new varieties of cloth produced to sell in them' (**71**, p. 82). Although Tudor monarchs consistently subordinated economic considerations to political ones of dynasty or defence, nevertheless Henry VII and Elizabeth did much to encourage this extension and diversification of English trade. They knew their power rested in part on a healthy economy; a flourishing overseas trade meant a high income from the customs and an increase in private shipbuilding which would in turn improve England's naval power.

3 Military Resources

England's military force under the Tudors was neither as well trained nor as well equipped as those on the Continent. Although there were some seasoned veterans within the ranks, the majority of soldiers were usually inexperienced in warfare. Their weapons, moreover, were out of date; lacking firearms and heavy horse, they relied too heavily on the bills and bows which had helped Henry V win at Agincourt a century before. Thus in the French campaign of 1544 barely one-tenth of the 28,000 infantrymen in the army had modern weapons, while apart from 50 Gentlemen Pensioners, there were singularly few men-at-arms (**58**).

In size, the English armies could bear comparison with the forces of Spain and France, at least during the early Tudor period. The 35,000-strong army which Henry VIII put into the field in 1513 matched in size any of those then fighting in Italy. European armies, however, were to become larger still as the sixteenth century progressed (**61, 63**). To try to keep pace imposed an enormous strain on England's resources of men, money and equipment. England's population was at most half that of Spain and a third that of France. The income of the English monarch was far below that of his European counterparts. To make matters even worse, the traditional means of recruiting armies for campaigns overseas was breaking down.

Early Tudor forces, like their medieval predecessors, were recruited in two ways and for two distinct functions. A national militia of able-bodied men was levied in the shires for the purposes of home defence against domestic rebellion and foreign invasion. A contract army was raised by nobles and gentlemen from their household servants, tenants and personal retainers mainly but not exclusively for overseas expeditions. This contract army had always been potentially dangerous to the Crown, as it placed military power in the hands of the nobility, but by the 1540s it was becoming very difficult to raise large armies by this means, as landowners were often unco-operative about mustering their retinues. Part of the problem may have been a natural resentment at providing troops for seemingly endless warfare; however, Dr Goring has convincingly suggested that the problem went deeper than this (99). He argues that the changing composition of the landowning class (due to the dissolution of the monasteries and the disappearance of some noble families) meant that the Crown was obliged to rely on a much wider group of landowners for raising troops. Some of these were obscure country gentlemen whose military resources were difficult for the government to assess accurately. Many of them were forced by inflation to reduce the size of their households and were thus unable to provide large bands of retainers for the Crown. Whatever the cause, the government found that it needed to turn to another source to supplement the troops levied from landowners' retinues.

The national militia was at hand and from 1544 took on some responsibility for recruiting men to be sent abroad. In this way and with the additional hire of foreign mercenaries some 40,000 soldiers were able to participate in the sieges of Boulogne and Montreuil in 1544 while 12,000 men were in Scotland (90, 99). There were, however, major weaknesses in using both systems for the same purpose. First, the national militia levied a force which was ill-equipped, wholly untrained and poorly organised. This was finally brought home to the government in January 1558 when, after severe problems in actually raising men in the counties for the relief of Calais, fewer than 200 of the 1000 assembled at Dover were found to have the proper equipment, and this was by no means unique (96). Secondly, recruiting men by two different but overlapping systems created administrative chaos. Once again it was the Calais campaign which fully exposed the problem. Sometimes commissioners for musters discovered that men on their lists had already been raised by private landowners for their own armies; sometimes they were hampered by landlords trying to keep back their tenants from service so that they might use them in their own bands at some later, and as yet unspecified, date (99).

The Calais débâcle stimulated Mary's 1558 parliament to introduce some reform of the muster system and the law for providing equipment; but it was left to the next reign to build on this foundation and overhaul the military machine. Under Elizabeth, the system was reformed in two major ways: first, a more effective command structure was developed in the counties under Lord Lieutenants; secondly, from the 1570s onwards regular training of the militia was carried out. In practice a unitary military organisation was developed. Although the Crown still used the landowners' retinues (for example, Leicester summoned his servants and dependants when embarking on the Netherlands campaign), it relied essentially on its bands of part-time, trained, well-armed militia men for its forces (**90, 96, 99**).

Such forces could not compete with those of Spain in the second half of the century. At best it was hoped that they could provide sufficient home defence in the event of invasion. Consequently, military adventures overseas on a large scale were out of the question. An important constraint on Elizabeth's foreign policy was her appreciation of the limitations of her army.

The navy, by contrast, grew in size and improved in standard during the Tudor period. Although Henry VII inherited about 7 royal ships in 1485 yet passed on only 5 to his son, he built, in fact, 5 new ships and captured 1. He also stimulated private ship-building by offering a royal bounty to subjects who built ships of over 80 tons and by encouraging trade through his so-called Navigation Acts of 1486 and 1489. Armaments were stored at Greenwich and Woolwich and the first royal-navy dry dock was completed at Portsmouth in 1497 (**90**).

Henry VIII's contribution to the navy was more ambitious: he built 46 new ships, bought 26 and captured 13, and at the end of his reign there were 53 royal ships, 28 of which were over 100 tons. The fire power of his ships was much greater, as guns began to be placed in the waists of ships to be fired through gun ports at long range. Dockyards were built at Woolwich and Deptford, and Portsmouth was enlarged. A Navy Board was established in 1546, with responsibility for all naval administration. Experienced and able men became in turn its chief working officer, the Treasurer of the Navy, and provided much of the impetus for new designs in shipping. William and Benjamin Gonson (1549–78) and Sir John Hawkins (1578–95) filled the office under the Tudors (**34, 76, 90, 112**). Under Northumberland, however, the royal navy was run down, as there was no money to build or even to repair ships. The number of big ships (400 to 1000 tons) fell from 12 in 1546 to 3 in 1554. It was Mary's marriage to Philip II that saved the navy from permanent decline (**97**). Philip needed English ships to guard the Channel from French privateers and thus protect this part of the route from Spain to the Netherlands. Consequently he urged the Privy Council to pursue an energetic naval policy. The war against the French provided the much-needed impetus for action: the organisation of the navy was improved and a shipbuilding programme was initiated, with the result that England emerged from the war with a well-led and better-managed navy, 'still undisputed ruler of the Narrow Seas'. Elizabeth thus had a sound base on which to build (**97, 98**).

Elizabeth, unlike her father, did not augment the number of ships in the royal navy. Instead, she relied heavily on private English shipping for her fleets. For example, in the 1589 naval expedition to Portugal, only 7 ships out of the fleet of 150 belonged to the Queen (**90, 114**). Elizabeth put up nearly half the capital, but privateers provided the actual ships in the hope of profit from plunder. Both private and royal ships improved in design and in fighting power, especially after the 1570s. The *Revenge* was the pride of its day but not unique in its ability to sink ships at long range and voyage across the oceans (**17, 25, 112**). The idea of the sea as a protective, though not complete, moat around England predated the Tudors. The loss of their lands in France, however, and the expansion of France into the Channel ports of Brittany and Picardy, brought home to Tudor Englishmen their vulnerability to attack and the need for a navy as a first line of defence (**86**). Under the early Tudors, no naval strategy had been developed and the navy was rarely used for offensive engagements. Then, during the French wars of 1543–63, privateering in the Channel became common, sanctioned by letters of marque* issued by the government. It was soon realised that great profits could be gained from such ventures for government and privateers alike. From 1564, the Queen and many of her councillors invested in and supported the privateering expeditions of captains like Hawkins and Drake who preyed upon Spanish and Portuguese shipping while making inroads into the Iberian Empire (**17, 107**) [**doc. 2b**].

The navy thus became transformed in two ways in the sixteenth century. From a coastal defence force, auxiliary to the army, it became an ocean-going, aggressive, striking power. From a small fleet which was reinforced in wartime by the hire of (usually foreign) vessels, the English navy became large but comprised royal and private shipping. Thus, whereas royal control over the army was virtually complete, over the navy it was weak. In consequence, though well armed, modern in design and a match for the Spaniards, the navy suffered from 'divergent aims and disunited commands' (**34; 90**, p. 135; **112**).

An active foreign policy required money as well as men. Munitions, fortifications, the wages of mercenaries had all to be paid for; and war was becoming an increasingly expensive business in the inflationary sixteenth century. The English monarchs simply did not have the ordinary resources to finance lengthy wars. Their ordinary revenues have been assessed at £100,000–150,000 which barely covered ordinary expenditure. Parliamentary taxation had to be levied but was inadequate for wartime needs, and so at times of war governments had to resort to expedients such as forced loans, sales of Crown lands, debasements of the currency and the sale of monopolies. Unlike the Kings of Spain and France, Tudor monarchs lacked the military resources to pursue an aggressive foreign policy without severely harming their own power and the economy of their country (**90**).

4 The Making of Foreign Policy

Foreign policy was the prerogative of monarchs. They could ask advice from councillors but were in no way bound by it [**doc. 3**]. Nevertheless, rarely were foreign-policy decisions taken without monarchs consulting the Privy Council or individual councillors informally. Conflicting views were frequently received on matters large and small, but while to some extent this gave monarchs freedom of action, they were usually cautious about pursuing ambitious policies without first winning over a substantial group of councillors. Thus, Mary did not yield to her husband's pleas that England should join Spain in its war against France until Stafford's raid had convinced the 'doves' in the Council of the inevitability of England's participation in the war. Similarly Elizabeth felt unable to marry the Duke of Anjou in 1579 because of the opposition from most of her councillors.

Parliament officially had no role to play in the making of foreign policy, although its power to vote or deny taxation might act as a restraining hand on a monarch who planned war. Yet parliament rarely resisted taxation; indeed it was rather the unwillingness of the country to pay taxes, sometimes already granted by parliament, that led the monarch on occasion to rethink his policies. The Cornish rebels in 1497, who protested against paying for the King's Scottish war, forced Henry VII to make a peace. Resistance to the unparliamentary 'Amicable Grant' in 1525 effectively sabotaged Henry VIII's plans for another invasion of France. Although these cases were exceptional, they were important in demonstrating the limitations of royal power to the monarchs themselves. When Elizabeth finally resorted to war against Spain, she showed a greater reluctance than her father to squeeze the country financially, perhaps because she feared popular insurrections (**90**). Elizabeth's respect for public opinion manifested itself in another significant way. From 1576 onwards, she allowed her privy councillors to place before parliament explanations of her policy in order to win parliamentary support and subsidies. Sir Walter Mildmay or Sir Christopher Hatton presented national security problems and an exposition of the government's policies to the Commons in 1576, 1581, 1584, 1585 and 1587. As Professor MacCaffrey has written, their speeches transformed foreign policy 'from an arcane preserve of the Crown into a topic of wide public concern' (**54**, p. 485). In 1587, however, the councillors clearly exceeded their instructions, when they tried to use parliament to put pressure on the Queen to accept the sovereignty of the Netherlands. Elizabeth had already rejected such an idea in Council and the councillors who favoured a forward policy in the Netherlands were trying to force the Queen to change her mind. Although the attempt failed, it 'casts a great deal of light on the winding intricacies of Elizabethan policy making' (**54**, p. 490).

Two further points need to be made about the formulation of foreign policy. The first is that decisions were frequently made on the basis of incomplete, biased and often inaccurate reports from diplomats abroad. The Tudor period saw a growth in diplomatic personnel and a greater bureaucratisation of the administration (**40, 57, 118**). Nevertheless, there were no career diplomats, and appointments were made in a rather haphazard way; language skills, experience overseas, but also the backing of a powerful patron, influenced most choices. Some of the choices were good, others were not, but the monarchs were dependent on ambassadors' reports to assess the situation abroad and determine policy. Another problem was that the reports of many reflected the views and interests of their patron. This was particularly important in the 1530s, when Cromwell chose the diplomatic staff and received personally most of the dispatches from abroad; and again in the 1570s and 1580s, when almost all men selected for special missions to the Netherlands and Germany were Leicester's protégés (**34, 84, 110**). In Mary's reign all overseas representatives, except for an agent in Rome, were Spanish appointees and doubled as Philip II's ambassadors (**49**).

The second point of interest is the influence which merchants and those investing in trade had on policy. More work needs to be carried out in this area, but even at the present state of research the merchant interest appears to be a steady, though by no means monolithic, pressure group. Under Henry VII London merchants encouraged the King to improve relations with the Burgundian court. Under Elizabeth, those involved in Iberian trade tried to encourage harmonious relations with Spain, whilst those investing in privateering did not flinch from confrontation or conflict with Spain. For example, Iberian merchants pressed the government to

The Background

restore Drake's spoils in 1580 to avoid a breach with Spain, whereas investors and sponsors of his voyage urged the government to keep the treasure (**17**). During the Spanish War, merchants suggested military strategies which reflected their economic interests, as when in 1589 a group of London merchants, among them leading promoters of privateering, put to the Privy Council a scheme for an exploratory three-ship voyage to India and the East Indies (**122**).

The making of foreign policy was thus a complex and intricate business. It was done on the basis of inadequate knowledge of European affairs and often in the face of conflicting advice. But for the historian one of the most difficult, if not insoluble, problems is to determine to what extent monarch or minister made policy. Was it Wolsey or Henry VIII, Cromwell or Henry VIII, Burghley or Elizabeth? The following analysis should help to provide some answers.

Part Two: Analysis

5 Henry VII 1485–1509

Introduction

Henry's foreign policy has been well examined in recent, readily accessible works and so there is no need to provide a detailed discussion here (**16, 22, 51, 81, 86**). Essentially his foreign policy was an extension of his domestic policy: to secure his dynasty by quelling plots of pretenders to the throne and by ensuring the succession through his descendants. England's interests, strategic and economic, were a secondary concern.

Policy of peace

Dynastic security depended heavily upon peace abroad. Wars could only be financed by heavy taxation which might well be resented by Henry's subjects. The Cornish insurrection against taxation levied in 1497 to secure the kingdom against a Scottish invasion was a painful reminder to Henry of the close link between foreign policy and domestic order. Furthermore, hostile courts abroad might provide a haven for Yorkist pretenders to the throne, whilst friendly rulers would recognise Henry's legitimacy, thus improving his credibility at home. Therefore Henry, from the moment of his accession, tried to secure alliances with the other princes. A one-year truce with France was proclaimed in October 1485 and was soon extended to last until January 1489. In 1486 Henry signed a three-year truce with Scotland and tried to arrange a marriage alliance between the two realms. In the same year a commercial treaty was made with the Duke of Brittany. Henry began negotiations for a marriage between his son, Arthur, and Catherine of Aragon in 1488, which was agreed in the Treaty of Medina del Campo the next year [**doc. 4**] (**22**). Henry strayed from his path of peace only during the Breton crisis of 1489–92. Yet even here he tried to use diplomacy rather than military action to resolve the problem. He first offered to mediate between the Duke of Brittany and Anne, Regent of France, who sought to annex the semi-autonomous duchy. It was only when the Duke died and Anne claimed the wardship of his 12-year-old heiress, also called Anne, that Henry felt compelled to offer official military aid to Brittany. Absorption of the duchy would provide France with a long coast-line on the other side of the Channel and, as Henry told a papal ambassador, this would pose a serious threat to England's security [**doc. 5**]. Yet Henry still tried to limit the extent of his military commitment. By the Treaty of Redon (1489) he agreed to send only 6000 men to the Duchess's aid and only on the condition that the Bretons paid their expenses. In addition, in order to share the burden of providing aid, Henry made alliances with Maximilian, King of the Romans, and Ferdinand of Aragon (**16, 86**).

The military campaign was a failure, for by 1491 Anne of Brittany had been married to Charles VIII of France, Maximilian had been bought off by France, while Ferdinand seemed apathetic about the future of the duchy. Henry VII was thus faced with a dilemma: either he could swallow his pride, accept France's victory and risk losing prestige at home and abroad; or he could fight with no allies and scant resources against a powerful France. In fact, Henry was able to tread a middle path which avoided both dangers. Announcing his claim to the throne of France, he landed at Calais in October 1492 with a substantial force and a few weeks later began to besiege Boulogne. Henry's purpose, however, was to negotiate from strength, not to enter a new Hundred Years' War. He had delayed the expedition for a year, and even then only set out when the campaigning season was nearly over, and he continued negotiating with the French throughout the crisis. Consequently he readily accepted the peace terms offered by Charles who wanted to be free to pursue adventures in Italy. On 3 November 1492, the Treaty of Étaples was concluded, in which Henry agreed to withdraw from France (save Calais) and Charles promised to pay an indemnity of about £159,000 in half-yearly instalments of £2,000 and to give no aid to Henry's rebels.

From then on the maintenance of good relations with France was a linchpin of Henry's foreign policy. Thus when he joined the Holy League, which was formed to combat French conquests in Italy, he made it clear that he had no intention of fighting against France, and the next year (1497) he signed a commercial treaty with Charles VIII. On the death of Charles in 1498, Henry refused to countenance the suggestion of Maximilian that they should launch a joint invasion against Louis XII. Similarly he would not agree to attack France when asked to do so by Ferdinand of Aragon in

1502. Although Henry always feared French designs on Flanders as a potential danger to England, he consistently avoided confrontation.

At the same time, Henry was able to continue his alliance with Spain. The Treaty of Medina del Campo was followed a decade later by a marriage alliance between Henry's heir, Arthur, and Catherine of Aragon. In October 1501, the couple were married in England. The Spanish alliance not only brought Henry the friendship of the most important power in Europe but also that of the Netherlands, since the heiress to Spain, Joanna, was married to Archduke Philip of Burgundy. Thus when Arthur died in April 1502 Henry was no less anxious than the Spanish monarchs were that the marriage alliance should be preserved. Within six months an English treaty was drafted to arrange for a marriage between the widowed Catherine and the new heir, Prince Henry. A formal treaty was signed in June 1503 but it decreed that the marriage should not take place until Prince Henry reached the age of 14 (**22**). From 1494 until 1504, at a time when the peace of Western Europe was shattered by the Italian Wars, Henry was thus able to remain on good terms with each of the main participants. They all sought his friendship in the hope that he might be induced to enter the wars on their side. Reports exaggerating his wealth and power made him appear a desirable ally [**doc. 6**].

Threats to the dynasty

Although Henry's dynastic policy led him to seek peaceful relations abroad, it also prevented him from playing the passive role in international affairs that he probably would have preferred. Henry had to pursue an active foreign policy in order to counter the danger of Yorkist conspiracies hatched or succoured overseas. The earliest plots – the Staffords' rising of 1486 and Lambert Simnel's imposture of 1487 – were not too serious; but the latter did indicate the problem of foreign support for conspiracies, as the Dowager Duchess Margaret of Burgundy, sister of Edward IV, had provided 2000 German mercenaries for the venture. Nevertheless Henry was able to suppress these risings without having to take action against Margaret.

Perkin Warbeck's activities, however, were more dangerous and influenced foreign policy decisions from his first impersonation as Richard, Duke of York, in the autumn of 1491 until his capture six years later. Warbeck had, at one time or another, the support of the Irish magnates, Charles VIII of France, James IV of Scotland, Margaret of Burgundy, her son-in-law, Maximilian, and her grandson, Philip of Burgundy. Apart from Duchess Margaret, who hated the 'usurper', Henry Tudor, these influential supporters of Warbeck used him merely as a pawn in diplomacy. They only gave Warbeck aid when they were antagonistic to Henry and hoped either to force the English King to follow their will or to replace him with a more pliable figure; and they were prepared to abandon Warbeck either in return for diplomatic concessions or if Henry proved too powerful to offend. Thus Charles VIII honoured Warbeck when he was experiencing difficulties with Henry over his plans to absorb Brittany into France. Maximilian allowed his mother-in-law to welcome Warbeck in 1492 because he was annoyed with Henry for making a separate peace with France, and in 1495 Maximilian resumed his patronage of Warbeck in order to 'encourage' Henry to join the Holy League. James IV helped Warbeck because of his designs on the fortress of Berwick held by the English since 1482 (**16, 51**).

Henry would not, however, submit to this kind of diplomatic pressure. Conscious of his insecure hold on his kingdom, he could not risk his credibility at home by adopting too weak and conciliatory a policy overseas. On the other hand he did not have the resources to mount full-scale expeditions against courts which harboured his enemies. Consequently he dealt with the danger of Perkin Warbeck by arresting suspected opponents at home, by sending Sir Edward Poynings to Ireland as Lord Deputy with an army, and by initiating diplomatic negotiations abroad, backed up where necessary by the threat of limited military intervention. He relied heavily on his friendship with Spain which had been forged in 1489 with the Treaty of Medina del Campo, and once peace had been reached with France at Étaples he relied on friendship from that quarter also. Both Spain and France had agreed by treaty not to protect Henry's enemies, and Henry sought to extract a similar promise from Scotland and the Burgundian government of the Netherlands. Duchess Margaret proved intransigent, however, and when Henry in 1493 imposed a trade embargo on the Low Countries in retaliation, the Burgundian government placed a counter-embargo on English trade and in December 1494 made a formal agreement with Warbeck. In 1495 Maximilian intimated that he would abandon Warbeck if Henry joined the Holy League, but as Henry refused to fight against France, Maximilian stepped up his support for Warbeck. However, the damage to the Netherlands' trade and the initiation of further negotiations to include Henry in the League convinced Maximilian and Philip of Burgundy that they had more to gain from the friendship of Henry than from that of Perkin Warbeck. Consequently, a commercial treaty was signed in February 1496, known later as the *Intercursus Magnus*, which included the stipulation that each government would not protect the other's rebels and that, if the Dowager Duchess Margaret would not follow this directive, she would lose her dower lands (**16, 86**).

James IV of Scotland was by 1496 the only ruler prepared to aid Warbeck, and in September his troops raided the English border on Warbeck's behalf in the hope that Englishmen would rise and proclaim him King. Parliament agreed to vote to levy an army against Scotland but a major tax revolt in Cornwall made Henry realise that a long campaign was out of the question. Even before 1496 Henry had offered James a marriage alliance to win his friendship. Now he renewed the offers with more success. After another abortive raid in 1497, when Scottish troops were repelled by an English army 10,000 strong, James was ready to come to terms. He sent Warbeck off in a Scottish ship to try his luck in Ireland and signed a seven-year truce with Henry at Ayton on 30 September. Soon afterwards this was extended into a marriage alliance when Henry's daughter, Margaret, was betrothed to James. The loss of this last courtly haven brought about the end of the Warbeck threat, and after a feeble attempt to stir a Yorkist rising in Ireland and Cornwall, the pretender surrendered to Henry.

The threats to the dynasty, however, did not die with the capitulation of Warbeck. Edmund de La Pole, Earl of Suffolk, and his brother Richard fled from Henry's court in 1501 and persuaded the Emperor Maximilian to give them support against Henry. The deaths of two of his sons had intensified Henry's sense of dynastic insecurity, for he showed even greater anxiety about the Poles than about Warbeck (**16, 47**). In 1504 Henry persuaded his parliament to renew the privileges and rights of the Hanse* since he remembered that Edward IV had recovered his throne in 1471 by means of Hanseatic support. Only when Henry secured custody of Suffolk, in 1506, did he revert to his earlier policy of eroding the Hanse's privileged position. Suffolk's capture was partly the result of chance. In 1506 a storm drove the ship of Philip of Burgundy and his wife to take refuge at a harbour in Dorset. Henry, taking advantage of this opportunity, welcomed the two at his court and signed a treaty of alliance with them. In the treaty, Philip promised to give no further aid to Henry's rebels and the following month he handed over Suffolk.

The last years

Henry's foreign policy during the last five or so years of his life had to respond to two major crises; the first threatened his dynasty, while the second endangered the pattern of friendships he had constructed so carefully. The deaths of Henry's two sons, Edmund (1500) and Arthur (1502), and of his wife, Elizabeth (1503), revived fears for the continuity of the Tudor dynasty. Henry now had only one male heir, Prince Henry, a boy of uncertain health and still only 11 years old in 1502. Henry's concern manifested itself in his arrest of two nephews of Edward IV and his ruthless treatment of potential traitors; fifty-one Acts of Attainder passed through the parliament of 1504. Another way of meeting the crisis was to marry and beget another heir. This Henry tried to do when he unsuccessfully sought the hand in turn of Queen Joanna of Naples, niece to Ferdinand of Aragon, Margaret of Savoy, daughter of Emperor Maximilian, and Joanna, widow of Philip of Burgundy who had died in 1506.

The death of Isabella of Castile in 1504 produced the second crisis. Her death ended the dynastic unity of Spain, as her husband Ferdinand, King of Aragon, had neither title nor power in Castile. Only if Joanna, heiress to Castile, allowed her father to act as Regent there until his own death, could the unity of the two Crowns be preserved. But Joanna's husband, Philip of Burgundy, insisted that she accept her inheritance immediately. Thus it looked as if Spain might disintegrate and Henry's powerful ally be reduced to a minor princeling. Henry could not afford to wait upon events. Prince Henry was supposed to marry Ferdinand's daughter, Catherine, in 1505, a marriage which was looking more and more like a *mésalliance*. Furthermore, France might take advantage of the situation and possibly reassert its claims to Flanders. Henry's response to the crisis was to draw closer to Maximilian and Philip of Burgundy. Commercial relations between England and Burgundy were of great importance, whereas Anglo-Spanish trade was minimal. Moreover, Philip of Burgundy seemed more likely to win the contest against his father-in-law, who was elderly and unpopular with the Castilian nobility. Finally, Henry's aid to Philip might be rewarded by the Burgundian surrender of the

Earl of Suffolk which would end the Yorkist conspiracy against his throne.

Thus, Henry was prepared to abandon the Spanish alliance which had up till then been a key element in his foreign policy. In June 1505 he arranged for Prince Henry to protest against the Spanish match before Bishop Fox, and he openly sought a French or Burgundian bride for his son. At the same time, he advanced huge sums to Philip to finance his expedition to Castile: £138,000 in 1505 alone. It was during this period of close co-operation with Burgundy that Philip and Joanna unexpectedly became Henry's guests after being driven by a storm into an English port (January 1506). The treaty which Henry was able to negotiate with Philip at that time offered English support to Joanna and arranged for Henry to marry Philip's sister, Margaret; before leaving, Philip agreed to hand over Suffolk and empowered several of his attendants to negotiate a trade alliance which was afterwards dubbed the *Intercursus Malus*.

But shortly after Philip had successfully taken control of Castile for Joanna, he died, and his wife (it was said) went mad with grief. Ferdinand of Aragon was able to regain power in Castile while Margaret of Savoy ruled the Netherlands as regent for her 6-year-old nephew, Archduke Charles. Henry's diplomacy was in shreds. Afraid that France might exploit the opportunity to seize land in Flanders, Henry tried to draw closer to Maximilian and repair links with Spain. As Margaret of Savoy had at last rejected his marriage proposal, Henry offered his hand to Joanna. He believed her 'madness' was mere propaganda on the part of Ferdinand who planned to rule in her place, and that Ferdinand would be pleased with the match since Joanna would thereafter be whisked off to England out of his way. Ferdinand, however, now that he was in control of Castile and allied to France, had no need to be reconciled with England. He would neither agree to Joanna's marriage nor send the remainder of the dowry of his daughter, Catherine, to England which would allow her marriage with Prince Henry to go ahead.

For the brief remainder of his life, Henry tried unsuccessfully to isolate Ferdinand. His daughter, Mary, married Archduke Charles by proxy in 1508, while negotiations were afoot for other marriage alliances with France and the Empire. But in December 1508, Spain joined the League of Cambrai against Venice – a league which included France, the Empire and the Papacy but not England (**16, 22, 86**).

Conclusion

Henry's foreign policy failed in detail; neither the expedition to
relieve Brittany, nor the attempts to isolate Ferdinand after 1507
were a success. His policy also proved expensive; between 1505 and
1509 he gave £342,000 in cash, plate or jewels to the Habsburgs
(**47**). Yet when Henry died, he left his country and dynasty inter-
nationally secure. There was no threat of foreign military intervention in England's internal affairs. Although England was not a
member of the League of Cambrai, its members were not hostile
to England and were preoccupied with Italy where no English
interests were at stake. European rulers respected Henry's power
and sought his friendship. Henry's success can be judged by
'comparing the extreme weakness of his international position in
1485 with its unspectacular but substantial strength towards the
end of his reign' (**22**, p. 273). This success was based on the firm
foundation of domestic strength and realistic objectives in foreign
policy.

6 Henry VIII

1509–14

At his accession, Henry VIII was bent on war. Brought up in a society where the chivalric ideal still counted for much and 'not unmindful that it was his duty to seek fame by military skill' (**11**, p. 161), the new King hoped to relive the glories of Agincourt and enter battle to recover his 'rightful' territories in France. It was no coincidence that one of his earliest actions was to commission a translation of a life of Henry V (**76**).

The international scene in 1509 did not present the opportunity for immediate war against France. At that time, the French King, Louis XII, was co-operating with the Empire, Spain and most of Italy in Pope Julius II's League of Cambrai against Venice. Henry's first task, therefore, was to effect the isolation of France. With this end in view, he sent Archbishop Bainbridge of York to Rome, both to reconcile the Venetians with the Pope and to encourage Julius to enter an alliance which would counter French influence in Italy. The mission was not difficult, as the Venetians had already suffered serious defeats and Julius was beginning to appreciate that the French were the main threat to papal independence. Bainbridge was consequently successful in helping to form a league against France in 1511 and, more importantly, in laying the foundations for a long period of Anglo-papal co-operation (**21, 88**).

Louis's response to the Pope's attempts to create a league against him was to summon a General Council of the Church* to Pisa. This act challenged the power of the Pope and thereby played into the hands of Julius, who could present his league as a holy one against a schismatic King. It also helped Henry to unite his Council behind war and in particular to overrule the clerical councillors, who had argued for a continuation of peace and had been responsible for the renewal of the Treaty of Étaples with France in 1510 (**76**). In November 1511 Henry and Ferdinand of Aragon agreed to mount a joint invasion against France on behalf of the Holy League, and decided to attack and conquer Guienne for Henry. However, while Spanish troops captured Navarre, the soldiers of the English army under Dorset mutinied or died of dysentery. The next year Henry tried his luck in Flanders, with Maximilian as his ally, and this campaign gave Henry the glory he craved. Under his leadership the army won a skirmish, grandiosely dubbed the Battle of the Spurs, destroyed the French fortress at Thérouanne and captured Tournai, which was a French enclave in Burgundian territory. 'The victory hath been so great that I think none hath been seen before', wrote Queen Catherine with more enthusiasm than accuracy, for the strategic value of Henry's gains was negligible (**27**, p. 118). Tournai, granted to England in the 1514 peace, was an expensive outpost, while it was the Emperor rather than Henry who benefited from the destruction of the French fortress at Thérouanne and the expulsion of the French from Tournai (**27**).

While Henry was enjoying the taste of war in Flanders, a far more important victory was won against the Scots. Relations between Henry and his brother-in-law, James IV, had deteriorated soon after the renewal of the 1502 Anglo-Scottish treaty at Henry's accession (**104**). By 1512 James IV was the ally of France and in the next year he crossed the border and seized Norham Castle in England. Meanwhile Catherine, governor of the realm in Henry's absence, and the Earl of Surrey raised 30,000–40,000 men to fight the Scots. There followed a massive defeat for Scotland at Flodden in September 1513 when the Scots lost their King and well over 10,000 men. 'This battle hath been to your grace and all your realm the greatest honour that could be, and more than ye should win the Crown of France, thanken be God for it,' wrote Catherine, with more accuracy than tact (**27**, p. 118). But the victory was not exploited, for instead of sending an English army to occupy Scotland, Henry merely left his sister there as Regent for the 17-month-old heir, in the hope that she would rule the country in his interests (**104**).

During the French war, Ferdinand and Maximilian had manipulated Henry into following a military strategy that was to their own, not to his, advantage. In 1514 Henry was again to be tricked by his allies. Although both had agreed to campaign with Henry against France before the end of 1514, Ferdinand first, then Maximilian, made separate peace with Louis XII. Consequently Henry was left to fight alone. As Louis had also come to terms with the new Pope, Leo X, Henry was soon persuaded, though reluctantly, to open negotiations with France. In August 1514 a peace treaty was signed which allowed Henry to keep his overseas gains and restored to him the French pensions, substantially augmented. A marriage between Henry's younger sister, Mary, and Louis was also arranged and took place in October. Thus, by the end of 1514, Henry had one sister as Queen of France and the other as Queen Regent of Scotland, but his treasury was almost empty and his territorial gains were insignificant.

Wolsey

Wolsey came to prominence and pre-eminence through the French war. His organisational skills had provided Henry with a well-equipped and relatively well-disciplined army in 1513. The King rewarded him with the bishoprics of Tournai and Lincoln in 1513. The next year Wolsey gave up Lincoln in return for the arch-bishopric of York, and in 1515 Henry appointed him Lord Chancellor. For the following fifteen years, Wolsey and Henry together made foreign policy. The extent of Wolsey's influence is undisputed, but there is considerable debate about his motives and aims.

In his biography of Wolsey, A. F. Pollard argued that the Cardinal aimed 'to hitch England to the Holy See' (**66**). When Rome sought peace, Wolsey followed suit; when Rome made war so did England. The reason for this subservience to Rome, decided Pollard, was Wolsey's personal ambition to become Cardinal, then Legate and finally Pope. This yearning for the papal tiara, he wrote, was 'the simple and straight thread' through the labyrinth of his foreign policy (**66**). A close scrutiny of the evidence, however, does not substantiate this thesis. First, England's good relations with the Papacy were more apparent than real. At times, England's foreign policy demonstrated independence, even opposition to papal designs; as for example when Wolsey sabotaged the papal initiative for a crusade in 1518 and superseded the Pope's sponsorship of a five-year general truce in Europe by the Treaty of London which brought glory to Henry and himself. In addition, Wolsey neglected to build up and cultivate a party of supporters in Rome, a task which should have been the first priority of any hopeful aspirant to the papal tiara. He did not go out to Rome, although he knew few curia cardinals personally. Nor did he try to secure favours or promotions for those lesser figures with whom he did work at the papal court. Furthermore, when the Papacy fell vacant in 1521 and 1523, Wolsey did not actively seek to fill the position but only reluctantly agreed to be a candidate when the King pressed him to put himself forward (**94**). Finally, there is a more general objection to Pollard's thesis. As Henry held strong opinions about the direction of foreign policy and often paid close attention to its detail, Wolsey could neither control policy nor dupe the King into following a course of action which was not seen to be in the royal interest. Nor would Wolsey try to, for he could not afford to offend the King on whom he was totally dependent for his power (**76**).

Henry's recent biographer, Professor J. J. Scarisbrick, offers a more generous explanation of Wolsey's aims. The Cardinal, he argues, sought peace throughout his political career; partly for the practical reason that 'war was the quickest way to lose money' but partly too because he was influenced by the New Learning and the humanist cries for an end to discord amongst princes (**76**). Thus, according to Scarisbrick, the Treaty of London, the tripartite conference at Calais and the meeting with Charles V at Bruges in 1521 were genuine attempts by Wolsey to bring about European peace. The fact that England went to war twice during Wolsey's period of political ascendancy, states Scarisbrick, was not evidence against this interpretation of his policy but merely a sign that his policy failed (**76**) [**doc. 7**]. This portrait of Wolsey as the humanist arbiter of peace is difficult to reconcile with the worldly pluralist who personified the abuses in the church condemned by humanists. Scarisbrick's Wolsey is a somewhat schizophrenic creature. A still more serious objection to Scarisbrick's thesis is that he takes Wolsey's own accounts of his actions at face value and accepts the sincerity of his protestations extolling the virtues of peace. Yet, if one looks behind the words, Wolsey does not seem to be bringing peace to Christendom; rather, he was actively trying before 1518 to check French power in Italy and after 1520 endeavouring to secure an Imperial alliance on the best possible terms.

The evidence is obviously open to many interpretations but the most convincing argument is expressed in Dana Scott Campbell's recent thesis on English diplomatic activity in this period (**118**). She argues that Wolsey was motivated to follow whatever course would bring him personal advancement and supreme power in England. Since his position depended entirely on the King, Wolsey had to keep royal favour by satisfying Henry's craving for glory and prestige within an international context. But as Wolsey's power could be enhanced if he received honours from the Pope, he was also keen to serve papal interests when they did not conflict with those of his master. As Archbishop of York, Wolsey was not primate of England; only by becoming permanent *legatus a latere** could he gain pre-eminence over all other churchmen in England and enjoy the extra-national prestige that would make him second to none (bar the King). Consequently, argues Campbell, Wolsey was led by his self-interest to promote the self-esteem of his King and where possible to follow the general direction of Rome. The following narrative is based on this interpretation of Wolsey's motives.

1515–26

The death of Louis XII on the last day of 1514 ended the brief *entente* between England and France. Mary Tudor, the royal widow, returned to England shortly afterwards as the wife of Charles Brandon, Duke of Suffolk, while the new French King, Francis I, aroused the jealousy of Henry by cutting a fine figure on the military field. At the battle of Marignano he defeated the renowned Swiss infantry and won Milan. Henry, unhappy at the emergence of such a dashing rival, was keen to build up a coalition against France. Wolsey speedily concluded an Anglo-Spanish treaty and dispatched Richard Pace as an envoy to hire Swiss troops who would fight alongside Maximilian and free Milan. Nevertheless Wolsey wanted to avoid open war at this juncture, since a parliament would have to be called to pay for it and the 1515 parliament had demonstrated alarming anti-clericalism. He therefore preferred to find allies to do the fighting (**86, 118**).

The death of Ferdinand of Aragon, however, led to a severe diplomatic setback for Henry and Wolsey. Ferdinand's successor, Archduke Charles of Burgundy, did not renew his grandfather's treaty with England but instead signed the Treaty of Noyon (1516) with the King of France. Soon afterwards, Maximilian too defected to the French camp and in 1517 concluded the Peace of Cambrai with Francis. Wolsey's diplomacy was in shreds. Not only had his plans for a new league against France ended, but also England was now diplomatically isolated. At the same time, Francis had demonstrated hostility to England by allowing the Duke of Albany, heir presumptive to the Scottish throne, to leave France and stir up trouble in Scotland. In these circumstances, Wolsey had little alternative but to repair relations with France. Anglo-French negotiations began in 1517 and an agreement was soon reached over maritime disputes and the problem of Scotland (**76, 86**).

Meanwhile, Pope Leo was anxious for a general European peace. Frightened by the westward advance of the Ottoman Turks, he argued that 'It is time that we woke from sleep lest we be put to the sword unawares' (**46**, p. 69). In this frame of mind, he despatched legates to the Empire, France, Spain and England to arrange for a five-year truce among Christian princes and a crusade against the Turks. Cardinal Campeggio was named legate for England. The time was thus opportune for England and the Papacy to work together; and as Anglo-papal co-operation could bring prestige to Henry and more substantial rewards for Wolsey, both exploited the opportunity to the utmost. First, they sought to secure for Wolsey the legatine commission which Leo had refused to grant for four years. Campeggio was denied admission to England until Leo, realising that his peace initiative would die if he did not give in, made Wolsey co-legate with Campeggio. Secondly, during Campeggio's stay, Wolsey continually upstaged and overshadowed the Cardinal in small but significant ways to take over the role of chief legate (**88**). Thirdly, Wolsey seized the diplomatic initiative and transformed the intended papal truce into an international treaty under his presidency. The Treaty of London which emerged in October 1518 was signed by all the major rulers and twenty lesser ones. They all pledged to keep the peace and to act together against any transgressor (**105**). It was a glittering success for Henry and Wolsey, whose fame as peacemakers spread throughout Europe [**doc. 7**]. Two days later, Henry concluded a treaty with French commissioners which settled most of the difficulties between the two realms: Tournai was ceded to France in return for another yearly pension; Wolsey was compensated for his loss of the episcopal see by a large sum; and Francis agreed to keep Albany out of Scotland. In addition, Henry's daughter, Mary, was promised in marriage to the Dauphin (**28, 88**).

As authors of the general peace, Henry and Wolsey were expected to remain impartial in future disputes. Therefore they could not take sides when, on Maximilian's death, Francis I and Charles of Spain and Burgundy stood as candidates in the Imperial election. Yet Henry's pride dictated that he act to prevent Francis from winning the election. Consequently, in the mistaken belief that the Pope would support him, Henry decided to present himself as a third candidate (**76, 118**). Charles won the election and thereby became the most powerful ruler in Europe. His victory also made him suzerain of Milan and a consequent threat to French control of that duchy. In these circumstances, the peace proclaimed at

London seemed unlikely to last. With war on the horizon, both Charles and Francis looked for a close understanding with Henry and each was keen to arrange a personal meeting with him. In the Treaty of London, plans had already been made for an audience between the English and French Kings, and a little later Wolsey had also extended an invitation to Charles to visit England. Now that both Francis and Charles were pressing for immediate talks, it was arranged that Henry should briefly see Charles in England, then sail to France for a longer meeting with Francis, and finally hold further discussions with Charles in Flanders in order to compensate for the brevity of the first meeting. In this way, Henry could display his even-handedness to both monarchs and continue to pose as the champion of peace, the role which had brought him such glory in 1518 (**118**). The meeting with Francis at the Field of the Cloth of Gold (June 1520) was a splendid chivalric occasion much to Henry's taste, despite the fact that he was worsted by Francis in a royal wrestling match. The discussions with Charles were more weighty and resulted in a treaty being signed in July 1520. This apparently committed Henry to very little, as he (and Charles) merely promised not to make any fresh alliances with Francis I for two years. Nevertheless, it did break the spirit of the Treaty of London and was viewed with suspicion by Francis (**46, 76, 86**).

The uneasy peace between Charles and Francis ended in 1521. During the previous autumn, Francis had taken advantage of a revolt within Spain to reconquer Spanish Navarre for the French family of Albret. At once Charles accused him of breaking the peace and appealed to Henry for help under the terms of the Treaty of London. Henry offered arbitration, which Charles accepted but Francis rejected. By the summer of 1521, however, Francis had suffered such military and diplomatic reverses that he was prepared after all to accept Henry VIII's offer of arbitration, and so a conference was arranged at Calais under Wolsey's chairmanship with no princes present (**46**). But Wolsey was now in no position to act as an impartial arbitrator since Henry had already decided to seek an Imperial alliance. Thus followed an extraordinary sequence of events.

The conference at Calais opened in August 1521, yet two days after the arrival of the French representatives, Wolsey left Calais for Bruges where he negotiated a treaty with Charles. By the treaty, Henry promised to declare war on France if the fighting continued until November and to mount a joint campaign with Charles in

May 1523. To cement their alliance, Henry's daughter, Mary, was to marry Charles instead of the Dauphin. From Bruges, Wolsey returned to Calais to carry on his pretence at arbitration. He may well have tried to negotiate a truce there and thus avoid the commitment to enter a war. But, as he probably realised, war was inevitable. In November Wolsey ended the talks as useless and England declared war on France (**76, 86, 100, 111**).

Henry's and Wolsey's motives in joining the Imperial camp are difficult to fathom. R. B. Wernham suggests that 'the explanation of Henry's undertaking to invade France with an army of 40,000 men is probably to be found in Charles's promise to marry Mary' (**86**, p. 102). Henry, thinks Wernham, was already worried about his failure to produce a son and wanted to marry his sole heiress to the strongest man in Europe. But Wernham's argument is unconvincing. As Henry knew, matrimonial agreements included in sixteenth-century treaties were often later overturned, and this dynastic arrangement was particularly fragile since Mary was too young to marry for several years. The attractions for Henry in forging an Imperial alliance lay elsewhere.

By 1521 it was clear that the peace negotiated at London would not last and that with it would disappear Henry's importance as an international peacemaker. Neutrality in the future war was not a policy to appeal to Henry, for it would reduce him to the role of onlooker in European affairs. An alliance with the Emperor, on the other hand, was a tempting proposition. Not only might it bring him further territorial gain in France but, even more importantly, it would assure him of the amity of the Pope. In 1521 Pope Leo made an alliance with Charles to free northern Italy from French influence and was encouraging Henry to reach an understanding with the Emperor. In consequence, Henry saw his alliance with the Emperor as part of a wider league – a kind of crusade – against the Pope's enemies; he saw himself as the saviour of Christendom. Wolsey was keen on the Imperial alliance for similar reasons, but he hoped for more material rewards, in particular a permanent legateship. Thus it was papal support for Charles that propelled Henry into war in 1522 (**118**).

Henry's war lost him any prestige he had hitherto enjoyed. The military expeditions into northern France under first Surrey then Suffolk, in 1522 and 1523, achieved little, but cost more than Henry could afford, nearly £40,000. In 1523 parliament had to be called to finance another campaign yet did not grant enough to allow

English armies to fight in France that year. Indeed, Wolsey was secretly negotiating for peace with the French government just before the decisive battle of Pavia when Charles V's army won Milan and captured Francis. Even Henry's attempt to gain some advantage from his ally's victory was foiled. When Henry heard news of Pavia he was delighted; 'Now is the time for the Emperor and myself to devise means of getting full satisfaction from France,' he declared [**doc. 9**]. Charles V, however, refused to countenance Henry's proposal for a joint invasion of France which would end in the total dismemberment of that kingdom. Nor would the taxpayers of England provide the funds necessary for such a venture; the so-called Amicable Grant provoked such opposition that Henry was forced to abandon it, and with it his grandiose scheme to invade France.

Throughout the war, Charles appeared to Henry as an unhelpful and untrustworthy ally. He had refused to release his troops from Italy and allow them to aid the English in northern France yet he had expected the English forces to march a long way south rather than seize some strategic points along the Channel coast. Then, in 1525, he refused his ally any fruits from the Imperial victory in Italy and at the same time he repudiated his marriage contract with Princess Mary.

No wonder Henry was ready by the summer of 1525 to withdraw from the Imperial alliance and make a separate peace with France. Wolsey also wanted peace, for the new Pope, Clement VII, alarmed by Charles's triumph at Pavia, had begun negotiating with the French government. Perhaps too, Wolsey had dreams of recovering the central role in diplomacy by organising an anti-Imperial league which would force the Emperor to make peace. This seems, at any rate, to have been the purpose of the Holy League of Cognac, concluded in May 1526, which had as members the Papacy, France, Venice and Florence. Henry VIII was protector but not a member as England could not afford to fight. Besides, Henry had other concerns. In the spring of 1527, alarmed about the succession to the English throne, he decided to divorce his wife and marry Anne Boleyn. Wolsey was entrusted with the task of using his diplomatic skills to bring about that end. At first, in the mistaken belief that Henry intended to marry a French princess, Wolsey fulfilled his duty enthusiastically; but then, when he realised Henry planned to marry into the anti-clerical Boleyn family, Wolsey carried out Henry's instructions with reluctance. Although it was not Wolsey's fault that the divorce was not obtained, the failure brought about his downfall, his arrest in November 1529 and possibly his premature death just before his trial.

Wolsey was a showman on a grand scale and, when he chose to be so, a very able administrator. For a short time he brought Henry to the forefront of the international scene. But the King did not have the military resources to preserve that position as Europe drifted into war. Furthermore, the political advantages of co-operating with the Pope evaporated as papal influence waned under the attack on its spiritual powers by the Lutherans, and on its territorial power through the Italian wars. Wolsey failed his master in 1525, and again in 1529, not because of any lack of skill but because England could only play at being a political giant. Neither he nor Henry could see that France and Spain were two leviathans with whom England could not compete. Their vision was clouded by their personal ambitions and unrealistic dreams.

1527–40

Once Henry had decided to divorce Catherine of Aragon in the spring of 1527, he devoted his diplomatic resources to that end and subordinated all other foreign policy considerations to his aim of securing papal agreement to his matrimonial plans. But the Pope's assent was not easy to obtain, for Clement VII was not a free agent. The sack of Rome by Imperial troops in May 1527 had left him a prisoner of Charles V, Catherine's nephew, who strongly opposed the divorce. Even after his release in December, Clement still needed the Emperor's goodwill to guarantee the independence of his territories. In order to combat Imperial power, Henry tried to enlist the aid of Francis I; first, to get Wolsey appointed papal regent while the Pope was in captivity, so that Wolsey could grant the necessary annulment; and secondly, when this plan failed because of Clement's release, to open a new military campaign and break Charles's control of Italy. At the same time, Henry sent embassy after embassy to Rome in search of a decretal commission which would empower Wolsey and a co-legate to try the divorce case in England without right of appeal on a point of law to the papal curia (**64, 88**).

Henry's policy was ultimately unsuccessful, for Francis I, though co-operative, was ineffective. Wolsey signed an agreement with Francis at Amiens in August 1527 and further Anglo-French talks took place at Compiègne soon afterwards. At the same time the

French launched an assault on Italy and, in support of Francis, Henry declared war on the Emperor in the following January. But the French military successes of 1528 swiftly turned to a series of defeats in 1529 (**46**). Given the uncertain political situation, Clement VII was unwilling to commit himself to granting a divorce. For two years he answered Henry's ambassadors with 'fair words and fair writings' but delivered nothing of any legal value (**76**). In May 1529 Henry lost patience with the Pope's prevarications and duplicity. Without waiting any longer for a watertight authority, he summoned a legatine court to hear his matrimonial case at Blackfriars, and the Pope was warned that its revocation to Rome would bring about the destruction of papal power in England. But Henry's timing was unfortunate. On 21 June French troops suffered an irreversible defeat at Landriano, which forced the Pope 'to become an Imperialist and to live and die as such' (**46**, p. 218). A week later he and Charles V signed the Treaty of Barcelona and, as a direct consequence, Henry's divorce case was revoked to Rome on 12 July. The Treaty of Cambrai (August) between Francis, the Emperor and the Pope cemented the Imperial-papal alliance and ended French military efforts in Italy. It was clear that Henry could not expect a favourable judgement when his divorce case was heard in Rome (**46, 64**). Accordingly, Henry worked hard to press the Pope not to hear the case at all. The Reformation Parliament was his main device, but his ambassadors abroad also had work to do. Royal agents in Rome were ordered to seek evidence from history that the Pope had no jurisdictional rights over the King of England. Henry's envoys successfully urged Francis I to send an embassy to the Pope on Henry's behalf. All to no avail. Clement, once so indecisive about the King's great matter, was now stiff in his resolve to hear the case at Rome. Henry sent Dr Edward Carne to Rome, as an 'excusator', to complain about the jurisdiction of the papal court (June 1530). Whether Henry's purpose was to obstruct the trial or to deny papal supremacy is irrelevant here, but the result was that Carne's activities delayed the hearing for two more years (**64, 76**).

In 1532 Henry thought it prudent to draw still closer to Francis I. It is not entirely clear whether he just wanted French cardinals to plead his cause at Rome or whether, as is more probable, he had already decided to break from Rome and thus needed French amity as a shield against papal and Imperial anger. Francis I responded positively to Henry's overtures; unwilling to accept as final the terms of Cambrai, which excluded him from Italy, he welcomed an alliance which could provide him with the means to close the Channel and cut off the Netherlands from Spain. But Francis also needed the Pope's friendship if he was to win back influence in Italy, and so he was trying to arrange a marriage between his son and the Pope's niece (**46**). The two Kings, therefore, worked at cross-purposes. Francis was seeking to reconcile Henry and the Pope by suggesting that Henry should marry Anne Boleyn in secret and then afterwards obtain the Pope's tacit consent – a proposal which ignored Henry's need for an indubitably legal heir. Henry was hoping to persuade Francis to approve of, perhaps even follow him into, schism; a hope which depended upon weaning Francis from his aspirations to control Italy and which was thus completely out of touch with Francis's priorities (**46, 76**). Nevertheless, the two Kings concluded a defensive alliance in June 1532, and in October they met at Boulogne and Calais. The French cardinals, Gramont and Tournon, were dispatched to work on Henry's behalf at Rome. But though these Franco-papal negotiations promised success, they went too slowly for Henry who, on discovering Anne's pregnancy in early January, married her publicly and proclaimed her Queen. Francis was furious at Henry's untimely action, while Henry was equally outraged when Francis pressed ahead with his marriage alliance and entertained the Pope for a month at Marseilles despite papal threats to excommunicate Henry. In fact the Franco-papal alliance was of advantage to Henry, for amongst other benefits it brought a delay in the sentence of excommunication (**46**).

Henry's breach with Rome and the attacks on papal supremacy in England, from 1533 to 1536, had revolutionary domestic repercussions. Their effects on the direction of foreign policy in the long term were far less fundamental but in the short term they severed the links between England and the Habsburgs and forced Henry to seek allies elsewhere. The greatest potential threat to Henry's marital and ecclesiastical policies clearly came from Charles V, who, it was feared, might use force to defend his religion, his aunt's rights, and his cousin Mary's claim to the throne. In fact, Charles was both unable and unwilling to intervene; the Turks and German protestants kept him busy elsewhere, whilst his concern that the Netherlands' economy would be badly damaged by an interruption of trade with England led him to ask the Pope in 1533 to refrain from placing an interdict on England, as that 'would disturb her intercourse with Spain and Flanders' (**65**, p. 248). Nevertheless, Henry looked around for allies against Charles and, as his relations

with Francis were still strained, his eye fell on the German protestants, some of whom had formed the military Schmalkaldic
League against the Emperor. Contacts with them had been made
as early as 1531, but negotiations did not become serious until
1533–34 when embassies were dispatched to Germany and Poland.
Although the agents sent on these missions – Christopher Mont,
Nicholas Heath, Robert Barnes and Stephen Vaughan – were all
close associates of Cromwell, it was Henry himself who initiated
this search for a protestant alliance (**34, 84**). His policy was not
a success. The only alliance that emerged from the considerable
diplomatic activity was an ill-conceived treaty with the revolutionary protestant government of Lübeck in 1534. Hoping to gain
some influence in the Baltic, Henry agreed to send ships, men and
money to help Lübeck place its own candidate on the disputed
throne of Denmark; but the policy had to be abandoned after a year
(**34, 84**). Elsewhere, the negotiations with protestants reached an
impasse by 1536. The Lutheran princes, remembering Henry's title
Fidei Defensor, did not trust Henry's motives in entering a schism
and demanded his subscription to the protestant Confession of
Augsburg as a preliminary to an alliance. Henry, for his part, was
prepared to forget that the Lutherans had not supported his arguments for the divorce or sanctioned his marriage to Anne, but was
unwilling to make any doctrinal concessions (**84**).

By 1536, when the negotiations lapsed, the need for allies did not
seem so acute. In that year, the renewal of fighting between Francis
and Charles freed England from the dangers of isolation while the
death of Catherine of Aragon both opened the way to an Anglo-
Imperial *rapprochement* and aroused hopes of a reconciliation with
the Pope. This sense of security was, however, short-lived. It was
dispelled by the seemingly impossible event of 1538 – the
conclusion of an amicable agreement between Francis and Charles.
At Nice, in June, they signed a ten-year truce, and a few months
later, at Aigues Mortes, they pledged themselves to co-operate
against the enemies of Christendom. An immediate freezing of
relations with England followed. In November, Charles raised
difficulties about a projected marriage between his niece, Christina,
and Henry. The next January, by the Pact of Toledo, Charles and
Francis agreed to sever connections with England, and a month
later they withdrew their ambassadors from London. At the same
time, Pope Paul III published his bull deposing Henry (which had
previously been suspended) and sent Cardinal Beaton to Scotland
and Cardinal Pole to France in order to rouse support for a Cath-

olic crusade (**34, 46, 86**). In reality, there was little danger of an invasion. Charles V had more pressing problems than that of Henry, Francis had no desire to act as a papal tool, whilst James V of Scotland was not prepared to make the first move. Perhaps most important, both Francis and Charles feared that the elimination of Henry would work to the other's advantage. But many in England believed the danger was real, though Henry himself seemed in less of a panic than his ministers, perhaps because he could not believe in the possibility of Charles and Francis working in concert for long. Nevertheless Henry reacted speedily on several fronts. The defences of the realm were put on an emergency footing at great cost to the Crown (paid for out of the 1539 dissolution of the monasteries). In order to avoid a Yorkist rising in defence of Roman Catholicism Henry either imprisoned or executed the remnants of the Pole family in 1538 and 1539. The Act of Six Articles was passed in parliament to reassure conservatives who were unhappy with the previous drift of religious change (**1, 76**). At the same time the hand of friendship was extended to any ruler at loggerheads with Charles V or the Pope: the Dukes of Urbino, Ferrara and Mantua, the King of Denmark, the Duke of Bavaria and the Princes of the Schmalkaldic League all received overtures from the King of England (**59, 84**).

Henry's rather ludicrous attempts to find himself a fourth wife in 1538 and 1539, and his subsequent marriage to Anne, sister of the Erastian Duke William of Cleves, were also responses to the national crisis. The Cleves marriage was not, as sometimes described, a policy designed by Cromwell as part of a grand protestant alliance; it was an expedient devised by Henry and Cromwell together as a means to end England's isolation. Only when Henry saw his intended bride did he seek to back out of the venture. 'If I had known as much before as I know now, she should have never come into this realm', he told Cromwell in disgust after his first viewing (**89**, p. 244). Had Charles V not been meeting Francis I in Paris the very day (1 January 1540) that Henry was meeting Anne, the marriage would probably not have taken place. But almost immediately after it was concluded the marriage became otiose, for England's relations with Francis soon improved. In February 1540 Norfolk had been sent to Paris to entice Francis away from his unnatural *entente* with Charles and tempt him back into his earlier role as protector of Charles's enemies. The mission proved a success and the Cleves marriage, already personally embarrassing to Henry, became not only politically embarrassing for Cromwell – who was wrongly identified as its instigator – but totally unnecessary for the security of the realm. It was even potentially dangerous as it might have drawn Henry into the maelstrom of German politics. No wonder Henry was so anxious to extricate himself from it, especially as his attention had already been caught by Catherine Howard (**59, 76, 89**).

The unfortunate Cleves marriage did not cause the fall of Cromwell in April 1540, as is sometimes suggested (**76**). Nevertheless it had affected Cromwell's fortunes adversely. It had made Henry lose confidence in his minister at a time when Cromwell's political position was being challenged by his rivals Norfolk and Gardiner, and perhaps too it had made Henry a prey to the charms of Catherine Howard, Norfolk's niece. Certainly Cromwell's reluctance to dissolve the Cleves marriage (because of Henry's choice for his fifth wife) shook the King's faith in his minister and made possible his fall (**34**).

Even before Cromwell's execution, it was clear that the threat of foreign invasion had passed. Charles and Francis were already quarrelling and it came as no great suprise when Charles invested his son with the duchy of Milan and another stage in the Habsburg–Valois wars began. Henry was thus freed to reconsider his objectives.

7   Mid-Tudor England 1540–63

Introduction

Over the last twenty years, the historiography of the mid-Tudor period has been a great growth area and the traditional description of the reigns of Edward and Mary as a time of crisis has been questioned. Initially some historians extended the time-scale of the mid-Tudor crisis to include the last years of Henry and the early part of Elizabeth's reign as they realised that many of the signs of weakness evident under Edward and Mary were also present from at least 1540 until 1563 (**43**). Now, however, the very designation 'mid-Tudor crisis' is being challenged and may very well soon fall into disuse. No longer are the middle decades of the sixteenth century described as a period of chronic instability, mismanagement and political conflict. Co-operation and constructive responses to problems are the themes emphasised by historians today (**83, 113**). Similarly some of the political leaders of the age have been reassessed. Somerset, traditionally described as the 'Good Duke', so unusually tolerant in his religious beliefs and enlightened in his social policies, is now seen as a figure more typical of his age in demanding religious uniformity as the linchpin of order, and a practical social programme of reform for political rather than idealistic ends (**44, 20**). Northumberland, too, has been transformed from an over-ambitious, generally disastrous factional leader into a statesman of great stature (**45, 19, 20, 92**). The focus of the new research has been mostly on the domestic, political scene rather than on the making of foreign policy. Nevertheless the reassessment of domestic politics has important implications for any discussion of England's relations with Europe.

In this section I have chosen to discuss together the mid-Tudor decades not because they represent a period of crisis when England's security was most vulnerable and government policies were unpopular and ill-considered. Rather, these years are discussed together because they mark the last time in the sixteenth century that the government embarked on Continental adventures in pursuit of dynastic interests. As such, they stand in stark contrast to the later reign of Elizabeth when for all practical purposes she gave up her intentions to acquire possessions in France (even though she did not renounce her claims formally). In addition these years saw a renewed interest and military involvement in the affairs of Scotland, providing a second element of continuity in foreign affairs across the mid-Tudor period.

1540–47

In October 1542 Henry's troops invaded Scotland; four months later Henry made a secret alliance with the Emperor which provided for a joint invasion of France within two years. In May 1544 the Earl of Hertford mounted a major punitive raid into Scotland; the following month an English army of 40,000 men arrived in France. A strong link between events in France and Scotland is thus clearly indicated; but the nature of the connection is by no means clear and has been variously interpreted by different historians.

According to A. F. Pollard, Henry's main purpose in foreign policy after 1540 was the conquest of Scotland. This was, he argued, part of a coherent policy of unification and imperialism. Henry had already declared himself emperor in his own kingdom by denying papal supremacy, had integrated Wales into the political system of England and had been crowned King of Ireland. Thus, only Scotland needed to be absorbed into England for Henry's vision of a united British Isles to be realised. The war against France, continued Pollard, was secondary to this greater purpose and was only made necessary by France's traditional friendship for Scotland and consequent aid to the Scots (**65**). Pollard's conclusion was based upon scholarly research, but it is no longer satisfactory in the light of modern interpretations of Henry's reign. In the first place, Henry is now seen as a traditionalist not an innovator; and in an age when political frontiers were the result of inheritance rather than geography it is unlikely that he was far-sighted enough to envisage the British Isles as a political entity. He certainly did not demonstrate the same prescience in his view of Calais; although geographically part of France, he never considered it as anything other than English. Moreover, the shiring of Wales and conversion of Ireland into a Kingdom were responses to specific political situations and not the working out of a grand design (**76**).

Perhaps because he is appreciative of these objections to Pollard's interpretation, R. B. Wernham has restated Pollard's idea in a different form. He re-emphasises the point that Henry's policy was directed primarily against Scotland but sees Henry's aims as fundamentally defensive. Scotland, linked by ties of friendship and marriage to France, was a great threat to England's security. Henry's fear was that James V would use his claim to the English throne (he was the son of Henry's elder sister) to throw England into confusion were Henry to die leaving under-age heirs. It was this security threat, not imperial dreams, that led Henry to seek mastery within the British Isles, thinks Wernham. Had Francis not planned to provide assistance to the Scots, he concludes, Henry would not have embarked on the war in France (**86**). J. J. Scarisbrick is not, however, convinced by Wernham's analysis. 'It is very arguable that concern for Scotland during the last years of his reign was secondary to his preoccupation with France and that, as in 1513, he looked to the North only because he was about to plunge into the continent' (**76**, p. 425). In other words Scarisbrick believes that the re-opening of the Habsburg–Valois wars in 1542 gave Henry his opportunity to return to the quest for military glory and territorial gain in France. The campaign against Scotland was but an attempt to fasten his backdoor before leaving for France.

Scarisbrick's scenario is very attractive. It is easy to imagine Henry, his manhood undermined by the revelations of the infidelities of his wife, Catherine Howard, seeking to regain his zest, dignity and glory by returning to his youthful dreams of conquest in France. Quite possibly too he was spurred on in his ambitions by younger courtiers who were restless for military adventure – and France provided much greater and more conventional opportunities for glory than Scotland. Nevertheless, as M. Bush has pointed out, 'Henry VIII's war against Scotland did not simply derive from his war against France'. Though the two wars were connected 'connection did not mean encapsulation'(**19**, p. 9). Just as it is a mistake to see the war against France as an offshoot of the Scottish war so it is wrong to assume that there would have been no war in Scotland had Henry not planned to fight against France. Henry had other motives for launching an attack on Scotland in 1542. During the dangerous years of the 1530s James V had demonstrated that, despite Henry's careful wooing of him, his loyalties were to France and Rome rather than to his English uncle. He had twice married French princesses, the second of whom, Mary of Guise, was being courted by Henry himself. He harboured the political rebels who fled to Scotland after the failure of the Pilgrimage of Grace. He ignored Henry's patronising advice to seize ecclesiastical lands and break with the Pope; instead Cardinal Beaton, an agent of the Pope, remained the most influential figure at James's court. Perhaps most important of all, James gravely insulted the English King when in September 1541 he failed to keep an appointment to meet Henry, then on his northern progress at York. Henry, who had been left waiting in vain for nine days, was predictably furious and no doubt determined to teach his young nephew a lesson (**101, 104**).

As a result, Henry sent ambassadors and an army of 3000 to the North in August 1542. These ambassadors presented humiliating demands to the Scots while the army stood in the wings, ready to act if the terms were not accepted. Although the Scots were in a conciliatory mood, their hesitation in accepting all the terms gave Henry the pretext to send his troops over the border. The raid was intended to intimidate and overawe James V but at first it had the opposite effect. James appealed to Rome for support and organised a force against England. The result was disastrous for Scotland. At Solway Moss, the Scots suffered an ignoble defeat; there were few casualties but many leading men were captured. Three weeks later James V died leaving the Scottish throne to his one-week-old daughter, Mary (**31, 76**). Had Henry so wanted, he could have easily invaded, conquered and incorporated Scotland into his kingdom. Why did he not do so? Wernham has argued that fear of the French deterred him from immediate action and that the amassing of ships, troops and supplies (intended for Scotland) at Rouen made Henry decide to take direct action against France rather than invade his northern neighbour (**86**). But in fact the number of French troops intended for Scotland was small; Paget, then ambassador to Paris, informed Henry, in January 1543, that 2000 men were destined to sail from Normandy (**37**). They were only a token gesture because the last thing Francis wanted was war with England just when he was preparing for action against Charles (**46**). This Henry surely realised, and if he had wanted to conquer Scotland the way was open for him. By this time, however, he was looking forward to resuming his military exploits in France and was negotiating an alliance with Charles V for this purpose. Consequently he preferred to subdue Scotland by other means – by a more circuitous route. He planned to use those Scottish lords captured at Solway Moss as the nucleus of a pro-English party in the Scottish government. They were liberated on the express understanding that they would bring

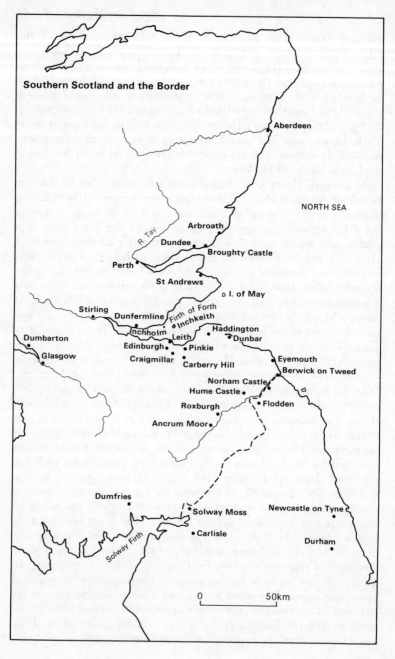

Southern Scotland and the Border

NORTH SEA

Aberdeen

R. Tay

Arbroath

Dundee

Broughty Castle

Perth

St Andrews

I. of May

Stirling

Dunfermline

Firth of Forth

Inchkeith

Inchholm

Leith

Haddington

Dumbarton

Edinburgh

Pinkie

Dunbar

Glasgow

Craigmillar

Carberry Hill

Eyemouth

Berwick on Tweed

Norham Castle

Hume Castle

Flodden

Roxburgh

Ancrum Moor

Dumfries

Newcastle on Tyne

Solway Moss

Carlisle

Durham

Solway Firth

0   50km

42

the Scottish Queen to England, arrange a dynastic union of the two realms through her marriage to Henry's heir, Edward, and act as Henry's agents in Scotland. Even after the Earl of Arran, heir presumptive to the Scottish throne, became governor in January 1543, Henry believed that he could control Scotland by means of his agents, for Arran seemed to be sympathetic to Henry's policies.

But Henry had misjudged the situation. His knowledge of Scottish affairs was slight and he did not heed the advice of those who were better informed [**doc. 10a**]. Sir Ralph Sadler, Henry's envoy in Edinburgh, warned him of the intensity of Scottish sentiment against an imposed union, explained the complexity of the Scottish political scene and pointed out the need to move cautiously (**77**). Yet Henry pressed hard for the young Queen Mary to be brought up in England, which merely aroused Scottish suspicions. He also had a misplaced confidence in the loyalty and power of Arran and the pro-English faction, and preferred threats to promises as a means of getting his own way. Consequently, the Treaties of Greenwich concluded in July 1543 formally betrothed the two children but did not bring Henry the immediate benefits of securing the custody of Mary and committing the Scots to the renunciation of all their alliances with France. As the summer progressed, opposition to the pro-English party grew in Scotland so that by August the country seemed on the brink of civil war, and in September Arran deserted the English cause. The final blow to Henry's policy came in December 1543, when the Scottish parliament repudiated the Treaties of Greenwich and renewed all previous treaties with France. In retaliation the King ordered his commander-in-chief, Edward Seymour, Earl of Hertford, to carry out a punitive raid into Scotland. Henry refused to occupy some strategic towns which would have helped him keep out the French and re-enter Scotland whenever he might choose, as Hertford advised. Instead he ordered Hertford to sack Edinburgh, Leith and St Andrews so that 'the upper stone be the nether and not one stick stand by another.' This Hertford had achieved by May (**1; 76**, p. 443) [**doc. 10b**].

Henry's decision to send only a small army into Scotland temporarily was the result of his concentration on the French war which by then was his main priority. Events in Scotland had prevented him launching a full-scale offensive into France in the summer of 1543. Only a small force of 5000 men under Sir John Wallop had entered the Boulonnais to help in the defence of the Low Countries. A major campaign was, however, planned for the

Analysis

summer of 1544. Thanks to the success of Hertford's raid it was set in motion in June, when over 40,000 men left for Calais. Henry's commitment to the venture is apparent from the manpower devoted to the enterprise. His enthusiasm can likewise be seen in his determination to be present with his army despite pressure from his councillors and the Imperial ambassador for him to stay safely at home. The campaign was shambolic even by the generous standards of the time, for Henry did not define his objectives until a full week after the vanguard of his army had arrived at Calais. Even before setting off, Henry had already begun to question the wisdom of the Anglo-Imperial strategy to march on Paris, but he had not yet decided what to do instead. Caution deterred him from advancing too far from his supply base in Calais, whilst greed led him to prefer to seize a piece of territory alongside the Calais Pale. At last, on 20 June, he ordered Norfolk to lead part of the army to besiege Montreuil; and a little later, Suffolk was sent to lay siege to Boulogne. Norfolk's army failed but Suffolk entered Boulogne on 18 September. Meanwhile, the Imperial troops, despite some setbacks, marched on through Champagne unchecked by French troops (except at the siege of Saint-Dizier and a skirmish near Soissons). Francis held his main army in reserve for the defence of Paris and tried to divide his enemies by extending unofficial peace-feelers to each. Henry for his part would listen to no peace proposals until he had captured Boulogne; but Charles, short of money and disappointed by Henry's independent actions, responded positively and signed the Treaty of Crépy with Francis on the same day as Boulogne surrendered to the English (**46, 76**).

Henry was thus left to continue the fight alone against France. Peace talks began in the autumn, and to Henry's chagrin Charles V acted as a mediator, but the negotiations broke down because of Henry's refusal to return Boulogne and his insistence that the French abandon the Scots. As an agreement thus seemed out of the question, Francis planned to attack the south coast of England, and send his troops to Scotland to facilitate an assault on England from the north. Henry's position looked exceedingly vulnerable. He had no allies, for his desperate approaches to the German princes had evoked little response and it looked as if the Catholic world would be united at a papal General Council due to assemble in December 1544. Furthermore, Henry's funds were running out and he had to fall back on further expropriation of church wealth and loans from Antwerp. 'England now faced a threat greater than that of 1539, greater than any, perhaps, she had known for generations, or would know again until Philip II threatened her,' wrote Scarisbrick (**76**, p. 454).

In fact the danger was a chimera. Francis, like Henry, could not afford a long, large-scale war. He probably had no intention of mounting an invasion of England. It is more likely that he planned to disrupt communications between England and Boulogne so that his army in Picardy could strike at and recapture the lost port. Charles V was preparing to fight the German protestants and would not become involved in the minor Anglo-French conflict (**46**).

On 31 May 1545 a French expeditionary force landed in Scotland where it was welcomed by the Scots, who were sickened by the destructive raids carried out regularly from England. On 16 July the French fleet left Le Havre and a few days later sailed into the Solent. In the skirmishes that followed, the *Mary Rose* sank with the loss of 500 men, not as the result of French guns but after water had poured through her open gun-ports. On 21 July the French landed on the Isle of Wight but only burned several villages before they were forced to withdraw. Another brief exchange of fire occurred near Beachy Head, after which the French retired to Le Havre. The French attempt to besiege Boulogne failed. Action on the Scottish front was equally uneventful; the Scots, after drawing close to the border, withdrew without doing any damage and Hertford carried out yet another punitive raid in the Lowlands (**46, 86**).

Both sides by September were keen to resume peace. In June 1546 the Treaty of Campe was signed whereby England was to retain Boulogne until 1554 when it was to be restored complete with the new fortifications built by the English, in return for 2 million *écus* to be paid by the French. In addition, France was to pay England all the pensions owed under former treaties. It was a compromise which was only acceptable to the two sides as a short-term measure because they could not afford to continue the fight. The treaty did not bring an immediate improvement of relations between the two countries. Lord Lisle, following oral instructions from his King, destroyed French fortifications near Boulogne after the treaty was signed. In November, Francis sent some help to Scotland when it looked as if Henry was about to mount another raid. Nevertheless, when Henry died in January 1547, an uneasy peace existed with both France and Scotland (**46, 76**).

Henry's last wars cost far more than those at the beginning of his reign, due partly to monetary inflation but more to their growing scale. According to the most reliable figures which have been compiled, the capture of Boulogne cost nearly £600,000 and its fortifications another £400,000. The war could not be financed by taxation alone; hence the heavy sale of Crown lands and feudal rights after 1540, the debasements of the coinage (1541–46) and the borrowing of large sums on the Antwerp money market from 1544. But not only Crown finance suffered. The wars resulted in a contraction of trade and contributed to the decay of old-established industries by starving them of capital investment. The increase in the pace of inflation in the mid-Tudor years also owed much to the war; both the debasement of the currency and increase in government expenditure worked to raise prices. Although the metal industries, especially the manufacture of cannon, were stimulated by the war and provided opportunities for employment, overall the wars had an adverse effect on the Crown's finances and the English economy. In short, in so far as there was an economic crisis in the 1540s, the war played a significant part in creating it (**30, 41, 90**).

Edward VI 1547–53

Henry VIII's death brought about a change of emphasis rather than a change of direction in foreign policy. Lord Protector Somerset (the erstwhile Earl of Hertford), like Henry, aimed at the dynastic union of Scotland and England through the marriage of Edward to Mary Stuart. Both men's purpose was to satisfy their honour and safeguard the kingdom; neither thought in idealistic terms of national consolidation. Somerset, like Henry, resorted to military action when the marriage policy failed, not in order to assert direct control of Scotland but to punish disobedience. Again like Henry, Somerset tried to win over a group of Scottish noblemen who might give 'assurances' of their support for the union. None the less, the Scottish war of Somerset differed in two vital respects from the wars of Henry. First, while Henry considered the Scottish problem as secondary to his concern with France, for Somerset the war against Scotland was the main priority. He thus sought peace with France to give himself a free hand in Scotland. Secondly, while Henry relied on a series of large-scale raids into Scotland to secure obedience, Somerset – who was only too aware of their military ineffectiveness since he had been responsible for executing them in Henry's reign – sought, instead, to place permanent military garrisons there as a means of enforcing his policy (**20**).

Initially Somerset tried to win his way in Scotland by negotiation. In late 1547 and early 1548 he made diplomatic overtures to individual Scottish lords but these were in the main unsuccessful. At the same time, he tried to encourage Protestantism in Scotland, a policy which also failed, possibly because he went about it in an unsustained, half-hearted way. Indeed how sincere Somerset was in these early attempts at a diplomatic, conciliatory solution is a matter of some debate (**20, 44**). It seems most likely that he went through the motions of non-military methods without having much faith in their successful outcome. He was certainly planning to use force at this time. Plans were afoot to establish military forts in Scotland. France was wooed in an attempt to keep her neutral. In March 1547 Francis I signed a treaty with Somerset, and on his death, discussions were opened with Henry II, his successor, about the sale of Boulogne before the stipulated date (1554) (**19**). But Henry II, more bellicose than his father, repudiated Francis's treaty and demanded not only the return of Boulogne but Calais too. The talks thus collapsed, for Somerset would not yield part of the King's patrimony (**121**). At the same time Somerset was trying to keep Charles V's friendship, since his goodwill was needed for the supply of foreign mercenaries from Flanders. Furthermore, should France aid the Scots, Somerset wanted to ensure that French ships would be unable to use the Netherlands' ports. With these ends in view, Somerset tried to present himself to the Imperial ambassador as a religious conservative and delayed the introduction of religious reform. Here his policy was more successful; Charles V was inclined to be friendly, and Anglo-Imperial amity deterred Henry II from declaring war on England immediately and sending a very large army to Scotland (**20**).

Nevertheless, Henry II was determined to prevent the pro-French party in Scotland from succumbing to English pressure. Accordingly, in June 1547 he dispatched Leo Strozzi there with a few thousand men and some artillery. These French reinforcements seized some military strongholds and it looked as if France would soon dominate Scotland. As a result, Somerset invaded with 18,000 men in September 1547. Although the Scots rallied, they suffered an overwhelming defeat at the battle of Pinkie. Now Somerset felt ready to implement fully his garrisoning policy; English garrisons were established on the islands of Inchholm and Inchkeith in the Firth of Forth, at Broughty Castle in the mouth of the Tay, and at Hume and Roxburgh Castles in the East Marches. By April 1548, Dundee, Arbroath, Dumfries and Haddington had been added to the list of garrison towns. The garrisons were intended as centres from which reprisal raids could be launched – as when Lord Grey (at Haddington) was ordered by Somerset to burn Lothian. But at the same time Somerset continued to try to win the friendship of the Scots. Tracts, such as the *Epistle to the Nobility of Scotland*, – which W. K. Jordan has used as evidence of Somerset's idealistic and moderate approach – were in fact pieces of propaganda produced at this time to justify the English government's policy. Bibles were distributed and preaching was encouraged to attract the Scots to the protestant and English cause. Ultimately, however, force became the order of the day because the Scots would not submit and the French arrived to give them aid (**20**).

After the battle of Pinkie, Henry II became increasingly concerned with the affairs of Scotland. He could not afford to see the disappearance of an ally and thus took up the status of 'Protector of Scotland'. In June 1548, 10,000 French troops landed in Scotland, occupied Edinburgh and carried off Mary Stuart to marry the Dauphin in France. Her arrival was greeted enthusiastically by Henry II who ostentatiously treated her as a daughter and boasted that France and Scotland were now one country (**121, 86**). Somerset did not adapt his Scottish policy to meet this major challenge from France. He simply hoped that Henry II would soon tire of the expense and pull out. Consequently he continued to rely on the policy of garrisoning instead of employing a naval blockade and invading once again with a large royal army. But although the garrisons were able to hold their own against the French, they were not large enough to defeat them or to provide sufficient protection for the Scots who had given 'assurances' to the English. By late 1548 the 'assured' Scots were changing allegiance and helping the French. To make matters worse, the garrisons were proving so expensive that an annual invasion would have cost less. Somerset spent over £351,000 in two years, which was almost double the cost of Henry VIII's five years of war in Scotland (**20**). Somerset had valued garrisons for their relative cheapness as well as their effectiveness, yet on both counts he was proved wrong.

Although French hostilities soon spilled over into the Boulonnais, Henry II did not declare war until August 1549. The summer risings in England, and Charles V's refusal in July to give assurances that he would help England to withstand any future French attack on Boulogne, dispelled Henry's earlier caution. The campaign itself was heavily influenced by the fact that Henry had delayed fighting until the summer, whereas the beginning of the campaigning season was usually in the spring. The French were unable to invest the forts around Boulogne until late August and the onset of heavy rains in early September put an end to the campaign without the recapture of the town.

The fall of Somerset in October 1549 made the Earl of Warwick (soon to be Duke of Northumberland) the dominant figure in the Council. Warwick's main aim was to restore order in the country and for this he needed peace abroad. Somerset himself had realised that the war had to be brought to an end, and it seems that he was about to open negotiations with the French when his Protectorate collapsed. Warwick, as early as November, decided to sell Boulogne and in this policy he had the support of Paget and other members of the Council (**108**). The issues for negotiation were how much the French would be prepared to pay for the town and whether Henry II would agree to continue paying the pension to the English King. The final treaty which emerged in January 1550 was described by W. K. Jordan as 'the most ignominious treaty signed by England during the century', the result of a policy of 'peace at any possible price' (**45**, p. 116). Many contemporaries too considered the treaty a blow to national pride; the contemporary allegory *Philargyrie* scorned Warwick for having 'sold for ready gold forts that were builded strong' (**43**, p. 165). Yet, D. L. Potter's recent thesis and article on the diplomacy of the peace have concluded that the treaty was not a French diktat; rather, that Henry II was forced to step down from the extreme demands he had initially made. For example, Henry had originally stipulated that he would only pay 150,000 *écus* for Boulogne yet 400,000 *écus* were finally agreed as his payment. Furthermore the treaty allowed the English to remove the equipment and munitions provided by them since 1544. The terms of the treaty therefore, argues Potter, while undoubtedly confirming the military advantages built up by the French in the two preceding years, were not the unmitigated disaster and humiliation for the English which might have been expected at the nadir of English fortunes during the summer of 1549 (**108, 121**). In matters of prestige, too, England's face was saved when a convenient formula was found to shelve the pension dispute. In fact the French pension was never again paid but the English did not concede their right to it. The treaty, moreover, was the only realistic outcome of a ruinous war which was causing financial collapse and internal instability. Finally, the abandoning of Boulogne relieved England from the financial strain of providing a considerable garrison there.

Northumberland's agreement with France at Angers in 1551 was a similarly realistic response to England's problems. Knowing that England could no longer afford to fight her ancient enemy, Northumberland was prepared to patch up a friendship in the hope that it would deter Henry II from attacking Calais. He did not sell England's interests for the price of maintaining his own personal ascendency at home, as Jordan suggests (**45**). Rather, he and his Council decided their first task must be to repair the damage wrought to the country's finances by the Scottish and French wars. Peace with France was the outcome; it may not have been glorious but it was expedient and with hindsight appears as an act of statesmanship (**19**).

Mary 1553–58

Mary's foreign policy has been customarily viewed as the most disastrous element in a disastrous reign. Her marriage to Philip II of Spain and the consequent Habsburg alliance provoked such bitter discord in England that they resulted in parliamentary protests, factional strife, one major rebellion and numerous conspiracies. England during her reign became the new battleground of Habsburg and Valois Kings, as the French and Spanish ambassadors competed for influence at the Marian court, while the French, after the Habsburg marriage, conspired with her enemies (**38, 50**). The alliance with Spain drew England into the final stage of the Italian Wars with the calamitous result of the loss of Calais. Even now, when Mary's reign is being presented in a more positive light, the traditional picture of her foreign policy has been little modified. In the essay on foreign policy in a recent volume reassessing mid-Tudor policy, C. S. L. Davies concludes that: 'Lack of enthusiasm for the war, lack of inspiration on Philip's part, bad leadership by the Council, bad morale, or worse, among the defenders of Calais, go a long way towards explaining the sorry results of the French War' (**96**, p. 185).

Mary's decision to marry Philip lay at the heart of her foreign policy. Yet the marriage was not as ill-conceived as hindsight suggests. Dynastic and religious considerations meant that Mary had to marry to produce a Catholic heir. Furthermore her sex suggested to contemporaries that she was not capable of ruling alone and needed a husband to share or remove the burdens of monarchy. Yet there were few eligible candidates for her hand; and only two were seriously considered, Edward Courtenay, Earl of Devon and of Yorkist descent, and the Archduke Philip, eldest son of Charles V. Though the preferred choice of the anti-Habsburgs, Courtenay was a man of little worth who has been subsequently condemned by most historians: 'his ambition was only exceeded by his lack of ability and his cowardice,' wrote one (**48**, p. 88); 'a very commonplace young man, easily persuaded or pushed in this direction or that,' wrote another (**68**, p. 208). There is nothing to indicate that he would have been a better choice for Mary. Philip, on the other hand, had much to recommend him as a husband. As Paget argued, England could use the Habsburg alliance as protection against Henry II of France who coveted Calais and had built up a strong Scottish alliance. Political stability might also be more easy to maintain with the promise of Imperial troops to suppress disorder whenever necessary. Commercial ties with the Netherlands made the marriage economic good sense (**37**). Mary's own determination to marry Philip, however, rested less on these political and economic considerations than on an emotional attachment to his father, Charles V. From the moment of her accession, Mary demonstrated the warmth of her feelings towards the Emperor, who had protected her during the reigns of her father and brother. In private audiences with the Imperial ambassador, she thanked Charles for his past help and promised him 'to follow your advice and choose whomsoever you might recommend' as a husband in the future (**5**, xi, p. 132). Charles seized the opportunity to press upon her the suit of his son, Philip, in order both to further Habsburg interests against France and, perhaps more importantly, to help Philip in asserting his claim to rule the Netherlands after Charles's death. The prestige of an English title and a power base in northern Europe would strengthen Philip's hand against the rival claims of Charles's brother and nephew.

The Habsburg marriage was thus a policy which can be defended as politically desirable as well as personally pleasing to the Queen. But Mary's method of negotiating the marriage was a mistake. Although there was little indication of fervent anti-Spanish feeling at the outset of her reign, Mary preferred to conduct the negotiations with the Imperial ambassador privately, even clandestinely, rather than openly in full Council. For three months the Council heard rumours of the match but they were not properly informed of Mary's intentions until 27 October 1553. During this period of uncertainty two political groupings arose at court: the one led by Paget in favour of the marriage; the other by Gardiner who opposed it and wanted the Queen to marry Courtenay. How severe the conflict was between the two groups is a matter of some debate

(**38, 50, 113**). The latest research argues that, at worst, there were only 'clamorous differences of opinion' (**113**, p. 60). Even if this is true (and the evidence is not clear-cut) the weight of Council opinion against the match probably did much to influence the thinking of lesser figures at court – men such as Croftes, Throgmorton, Carew and Wyatt who became prepared to rebel as a means to thwart the marriage. Furthermore, the manner in which Mary had closeted herself with the Imperial ambassador lent substance to the fears that Mary would in future listen to Spanish advisers instead of to deserving Englishmen. The strong opposition to the marriage came as something of a surprise to some observers and is indeed difficult to explain. Renard, the Spanish ambassador, told Philip that antipathy to Spain had been provoked by the intrigues of the French, the heretics and the nobility who favoured Courtenay [**doc. 12**]. Paget believed that the antipathy stemmed from 'the fears entertained by the English that his Highness, if the Queen were to die without heirs, might try to make himself King of England' (**5**, xi, p. 393). There was also the natural concern in a male-dominated society that Mary would defer all decisions to her husband and that consequently Englishmen would be excluded from patronage, and that England would be drawn into the war against France.

The marriage treaty allayed some of these fears – although there was always the danger that Philip would not abide by it. While Mary lived, Philip's powers were strictly curtailed within the realm. It was explicitly stated that 'The Realm of England by occasion of this matrimony, shall not directly or indirectly be tangled with the war that is' (**96**, p. 160). If Mary were to die without issue, Philip's titles and rights would die with her, but if Mary produced a son, he would inherit England, the Netherlands and Franche-Comté. Spain would also be his, if Philip's son by an earlier marriage died without heirs. Such a favourable treaty was drawn up by the English Council; so it seems clear that far from being paralysed into inactivity by dissensions about the marriage, the opposition within the Council to the Habsburg was channelled constructively into devising safeguards to protect the realm against a Spanish King (**113**).

The worst of the opposition to the marriage was over by February 1554. Neither French interference nor English protests could prevent Philip's safe arrival in July 1554 and the marriage ceremony on the 25th. It is true that anti-Habsburg sentiment did not subside after the wedding and expressed itself in propaganda (e.g., *A Warnyng for England*), tumults and parliamentary opposition to Philip's coronation (**6**). Yet it should not be exaggerated; after the failure of Wyatt's rebellion, no further rebellion shook the reign. Divisions within the Council centred on ecclesiastical matters rather than on foreign policy or Philip's powers in England; and although English malcontents, such as Henry Dudley and the Killigrew brothers, clustered around the French court and plotted the deposition of Mary, their plots were foiled with ease (**50**).

The marriage did not at first have a great impact on foreign policy, for Mary, like her councillors and subjects, had no wish to go to war. Consequently, to avoid the obligation to fight for her husband's cause, she sent Paget and Gardiner to La Marque near Calais in May 1555 to arrange a general peace. Although this attempt at mediation failed, France and Spain patched up their differences at Vaucelles in February 1556, when they signed a five-year truce without involving England in the negotiations. The Truce of Vaucelles was treated by the English Council as a calculated snub but in fact it brought Mary some benefit. Henry II of France's enthusiasm for the plots of Dudley and his fellow conspirators noticeably waned as the danger of war with England subsided; and this partly explains their failure (**50**).

But the truce lasted only a short while. Conflict between the Pope and Imperialists in Italy led to military action there in September, and the Duke of Guise soon afterwards set out for Italy with a French army to help his ally, the Pope. When in January 1557 the French breached the truce in Flanders, Philip called for English aid. On such an important issue Mary could not act alone without consulting her Council. The councillors came out unequivocally against intervention: it was against the terms of the marriage treaty, they argued; the country could not afford a war; and the threat of sedition made it 'very daungerous to entangle them now with new warres especially where necessitie of defence shall not require the same' (**49**, p. 242). Philip, however, was determined to obtain England's full support and arrived in England in March to achieve that end. Paget had already declared himself in favour of the war, but only three or four councillors supported him and Philip had great difficulty in winning others over. It was only the raid on Scarborough Castle at the end of April by Thomas Stafford and the exiles from France that induced the Council to change its mind. Indeed so fortunate were the timing and results of Stafford's raid that D. M. Loades has wondered if 'Stafford's apparently harebrained and provocative venture was not connived at or even prompted by Paget and his agents' (**49**, p. 367). Henry II certainly disclaimed any responsibility for such a misconceived adventure: 'I bade him [i.e. Stafford] beware as I already saw him without his head if he persisted in these ideas of his' (**68**, p. 353).

'Seldom, if ever, has England gone to war so unwilling and so unprepared,' writes R. B. Wernham (**86**, p. 231). In fact, once war was declared, the Queen's subjects rallied around the government. Those who had been implicated in rebellion or sedition willingly took commands in the army and navy. Sir Peter Carew, Sir James Croftes, Sir Nicholas Throgmorton, William Winter and the three sons of the Duke of Northumberland were but a few of the ex-conspirators who fought for Mary in 1557 (**96, 97**). The difficulties experienced in raising troops were the result of both the inefficient muster system and the famine of 1555–57 rather than a reflection of popular hostility to the war. Although there were men who refused to pay the 1557 forced loan, £109,000 was collected by it – an amount not much lower than the sums brought in by each of Henry VIII's forced loans in the 1540s. The parliamentary subsidy of 1558 raised £168,000 which was as much as the government had wanted, and the objections voiced in that parliament were not to voting supply in itself but to committing the country in advance to taxation for 1559 (**96, 120**).

The fighting at first went well. On the Continent a small English force under Pembroke took part in the successful siege of Saint-Quentin in August, and although it arrived after the worst of the fighting, its performance attracted favourable comment. On the Scottish borders, Shrewsbury was able to contain minor incursions and the Scots failed to respond to Henry II's call for an invasion of England [**doc. 13**]. By October 1557 the campaign seemed over; the Pope had accepted the Spanish terms and Philip's army was preparing for winter. But the dry weather continued and Henry II decided to try to recoup his prestige after the humiliation of Saint-Quentin by an enterprise against Calais. He recalled the Duke of Guise from Italy, and in January 1558 Guise's army attacked and captured Calais within eight days [**doc. 14**]. Many explanations have been postulated for the speedy fall of the fortress. Responsibility immediately fell on the deputy of Calais, Lord Wentworth. He was charged with (and in 1559 acquitted of) treason. Although he can justly be accused of undue complacency in the face of danger, he did not betray the garrison to the French. Mary's economy drive has also been held to blame for the disaster; the castle of Calais was in need of repair although the outer defences were satisfactory. More importantly the garrison was run down after August to save money. It was thus only at peacetime strength when assaulted, and contained barely half the number required for minimum security against attack. To counteract Guise's invasion, therefore, reinforcements were needed, but these were not forthcoming as the Council, unable to believe that Calais was seriously threatened, failed to send a relief army to Wentworth before 1 January. Philip, too, did not order his army to aid Calais; he only sent 200 arquebusiers on 6 January (**96**).

Calais, once lost, could have been recaptured. Indeed Philip urged a military effort to recover the Pale and offered to use his own Netherlands' army in the campaign. By this time, however, the Council was too demoralised to respond positively. The financial cost, the difficulty of raising troops, fear of attack from Scotland were all arguments put forward to reject Philip's plan. The Council's co-operativeness was possibly not helped by the fact that the Spaniards' payment of English pensions was 10,000 ducats in arrears. Furthermore, the Council had other grievances against Philip II. He had refused to sever relations with the Scots at the time when a Scottish invasion seemed imminent. Nor would he assist the Merchant Adventurers in their periodic quarrels with the Hanseatic League; on the contrary he wanted to uphold the League's claims to privileges which were unacceptable to the English Council. Other seemingly trivial disputes also served to convince the councillors that Philip had no concern for English interests and that they in turn should not sink their resources into another campaign on behalf of Spain (**5, 49, 96**).

The war, none the less, continued. Though the recapture of Calais was not attempted, a large-scale attack was mounted against Brest in the summer, but this failed dismally. Peace negotiations began in May and by October it was becoming clear that a settlement would be reached which left Calais in French hands. Before a treaty was drawn up, Mary died and the peace conference was adjourned until her successor was crowned. Philip followed the terms of the marriage settlement, withdrew gracefully from his English title and allowed Elizabeth to inherit the throne. The fears of the opponents of the marriage, therefore, were unrealised.

Elizabeth I 1558–63

Elizabeth inherited a realm which seemed especially vulnerable to attack. Although peace negotiations had begun at Câteau-

Cambrésis, France and England were still technically at war, while French troops were in Scotland and the French Dauphiness, Mary Stuart, declared herself to be the legitimate Catholic claimant to the English throne. The Pope had already declared Elizabeth a bastard, thereby giving the French a mandate to invade (**6**). Elizabeth was consequently dependent on England's alliance with Spain as a means of protection. The Spanish alliance was, however, by no means sure. Philip might make a separate peace with France and, if the Pope went on to excommunicate Elizabeth, even join in a crusade against her. Nevertheless, Elizabeth thought that she could rely on Philip's support. Her diplomats assured her that it was against Spanish interests for the French-backed Mary Stuart to replace her as Queen of England – and they were right. 'If England were lost, it cannot convincingly be denied, though some would dispute it, that these lands of Flanders themselves would be in imminent danger,' argued a policy directive written for Philip in 1559 (**42**, p. 50). Consequently, despite Elizabeth's early demonstrations of committed protestantism, there was a strong basis for Anglo-Spanish co-operation, and Philip promised to safeguard English interests in the peace negotiations reopening in February at Câteau-Cambrésis. The main stumbling block to peace was the future of Calais, since Elizabeth would not agree to accept its humiliating loss. But after a month of fruitless discussion, Henry II offered a face-saving formula which Elizabeth could accept: the French would hold Calais for eight years and then would either return it to England or pay a sum in compensation. Henry also made other concessions: he agreed to include Scotland in the treaty and to pull down the fortress of Eyemouth on the Scottish borders. The Treaty of Câteau-Cambrésis was signed on 2 April 1559. According to the late Sir John Neale, its conclusion freed Elizabeth from the necessity of appearing conservative in religion in order to keep the Spanish alliance and allowed her subsequently to permit a full reformation of the English church. A review of the evidence by Norman Jones, however, has shown that the signing of the treaty had no influence on the making of her religious settlement. Nor did the Elizabethan church settlement have any immediate impact on relations with Spain, for Philip continued to protect Elizabeth at the papal court and to seek a Habsburg marriage alliance with her (**60, 42**).

Furthermore the conclusion of peace did not greatly improve relations with France. Henry II continued to uphold his daughter-in-law's claim to the English throne and strengthened French influence in Scotland. Consequently, many of Elizabeth's councillors were delighted at the news that Scottish protestant nobles had rebelled against the pro-French and Catholic policies of the Regent, Mary of Guise, in 1559. The Queen's Secretary, William Cecil, in particular, wanted to help the Scottish rebels in order to scupper the French and protect the realm; and he was largely responsible for the escape of the Earl of Arran (son of the Duke of Châtelherault, heir presumptive to the Scottish throne) from captivity in France so that Châtelherault might feel free to lead the opposition against the Regent. Cecil favoured military aid for the rebels but Elizabeth herself was more cautious [**doc. 3(b)**]. Although she allowed warm messages of support and £2,000 to be sent to the protestant lords, she refused to countenance the deposing of Mary or the dispatch of an army to Scotland. Paramount in her mind was the maxim: 'It is against God's law to aid any subjects against their natural prince' (**86**).

Developments in France, however, forced her hand. The death of Henry II in July brought Mary Stuart to the French throne as the wife of Francis II. Her uncles, the Duke of Guise and the Cardinal of Lorraine, dominated the new King and were determined to stamp out the rebellion in Scotland and assert Mary's claim to England. In August and September they sent 2000 French soldiers to Scotland while Elboeuf (another Guise) stood by ready to send a further 8000 or 10,000 men as necessary. The Scots, powerless against the French, appealed to Elizabeth for aid (**79**).

In December 1559 the Council met to discuss the question. Cecil, naturally, supported military action to assist the protestant lords, and Pembroke, Clinton, Howard and some others agreed with him. Nicholas Bacon, however, led a group who feared the dangers of war against France and preferred to give secret, indirect aid; whilst the Duke of Norfolk argued that Elizabeth should marry an Archduke of Austria and enjoy the security of a Habsburg alliance against France instead of dabbling in Scottish politics (**53, 82**). Elizabeth was still reluctant to commit herself openly to the rebels whose protestantism and politics were too radical for her tastes. Only the news in late December that the French troops had reached Leith persuaded her and the more conservative councillors to act. On 27 December Admiral Winter was sent to the Firth of Forth, ostensibly to seek out pirates but in reality to blockade the French at Leith. Military intervention was ruled out for the time being until the outcome of Winter's mission could be assessed (**53, 82, 86**).

Analysis

Soon it became clear that more than a naval blockade would be required to flush out the French. Elizabeth therefore agreed at the Treaty of Berwick in February 1560 to give the Scottish lords protection, but 'only for the preservation of the same in their old freedoms and liberties from conquest during the time that the marriage shall continue betwixt the Queen of Scots and the French King and one year after' (**86**, p. 255). At the end of March, Lord Grey led English troops into Scotland and moved against the French stronghold at Leith. The siege went on until June when the French agreed to negotiate. On 6 July, English and French commissioners signed the Treaty of Edinburgh which provided for the withdrawal of both English and French forces from Scotland and the renunciation of Mary's right to use the English arms and title (**32, 86**). It remained unratified by Mary Stuart.

Cecil's adventurous policy had thus paid dividends and the subsequent establishment of protestantism in Scotland effectively closed that country to French influence until the end of the decade. Elizabeth's caution had also contributed to the successful outcome. She had effectively, if unknowingly, delayed military intervention until a propitious time, when Guise power in France was being challenged by the Huguenots. The result was that the Guises were prepared to make terms with Elizabeth in order to concentrate on their problems at home.

The political struggles faced by the Guises in France gave England security for the next year. The death of Francis II and the seizure of the regency by Catherine de Medici brought moderates to power who had no wish for a conflict with England. In March 1562, however, civil war broke out in France and by July it looked as though the Guises would triumph. In desperation Huguenot* leaders pleaded for Elizabeth's aid, and offered in return immediate possession of Dieppe and Le Havre as pledges for the eventual cession of Calais. Elizabeth demonstrated no signs of the hesitation and reluctance to act which she had displayed in 1559. She had been unhappy at accepting the loss of Calais at Câteau-Cambrésis and had unsuccessfully tried to reopen negotiations for its future at the Edinburgh talks in 1560 (her instructions arrived after the treaty had been signed). The possible recovery of Calais attracted her to the Huguenot cause at least as much as the fear of a Guise victory [**doc. 15b**]. For her councillors the issues were different; Cecil was most concerned with the security angle [**doc. 15a**]; Robert Dudley, the Queen's influential favourite, supported an interventionist policy to forward his own political ambitions. But although their priorities might have differed, the Queen and Council were agreed on a policy of military aid to the Huguenots. By the Treaty of Hampton Court (September 1562) Elizabeth promised loans and troops to the Huguenots (**53**).

The war went badly for England. First Rouen and then Dieppe fell to the Catholics before the end of the year. The final humiliation came when the Huguenot leader, Condé, patched up his disagreements with Catherine de Medici and agreed to help her expel the English from France. On 29 June 1563 the English garrison at Le Havre surrendered, and with it went Elizabeth's hopes for the recovery of Calais. Thereafter national defence, rather than dynastic gains, became the order of the day.

8 Elizabeth I 1564–1603

Spain 1564–85

For the first decade of Elizabeth's reign, England's relations with Spain were uneasy but not especially strained. Neither Philip nor Elizabeth wanted to sever the traditional Anglo-Habsburg friendship. Philip II, for all his Catholicism, preferred a heretic to a French woman as Queen of England and thus twice during the 1560s dissuaded the Pope from excommunicating Elizabeth. Elizabeth, for her part, wanted peace with Spain to counteract the danger of hostility from the Guises in France. Consequently, despite minor disagreements between the English and Netherlands' governments over trade and politics which culminated in the trade embargo of 1564, there was no open breach between England and Spain before 1568. Cordial relations were greatly assisted by the presence of De Silva as Spanish ambassador at Elizabeth's court from 1564 to 1568, a man who was greatly liked by the Queen and adept at smoothing over minor irritations (**33, 71**).

The breach of 1568 was not the result of a new hard-line Catholic attitude in Spain towards England. Despite appearances to the contrary, the expulsion of John Man, the English ambassador, from the Spanish court in April and the replacement in September of De Silva by De Spes, a friend of English Catholic exiles, should not be taken as signs of a new direction in Spanish foreign policy. Dr Man, a married protestant cleric, who was reported to have called the Pope 'a canting little monk', was hardly a wise choice of diplomat for Spain and it was perhaps surprising that Philip tolerated him for three years. Similarly, the transfer of De Silva to Venice was requested by the ambassador himself; four years was a long time to spend in such an arduous and expensive posting as ambassador to England (**33, 87**).

The origins of the breakdown in Anglo-Spanish relations lay in the events occurring in the Netherlands between 1566 and 1568. Whereas under Charles V the Netherlands had been a loose dynastic confederation of semi-autonomous provinces and cities, under Philip II more centralised rule was imposed. When a revolt broke out in 1566, Philip responded by sending the Duke of Alva with an army of 10,000 men, later augmented to 50,000, to suppress it. Elizabeth's attitude to this turn of events was ambivalent. On the one hand her dislike of rebels led her to approve publicly the executions of the principals, Egmont and Horn. On the other, she perceived grave security dangers in the presence of Spanish troops in the Netherlands; for the deep harbours and the prevailing winds made that country an excellent springboard for an invasion of England, and once Alva completed his task of restoring order and extirpating heresy he might well be tempted to try such a venture (**86**).

By the end of 1568 a crisis was approaching; Alva had achieved a military victory over all his opponents including Louis of Nassau and William of Orange. There were few options open to Elizabeth to combat this danger to England's security. War was out of the question for England did not have the military power to face Alva on equal terms, and the dangers of sending a small force to aid the Netherlanders were apparent to anyone remembering the 1562–63 fiasco in France. Harassment of Spain may have seemed the only viable policy. One method of harassment was to encourage the attempts of seamen to break through the Spanish trading monopoly, and perhaps Hawkins's voyages should be seen in this light [**doc. 2b**]. John Hawkins, who made three voyages in 1563, 1565 and 1567, sailed to West Africa, purchased or seized slaves there and sold them in Spanish America. In so doing, he was breaking the trading monopoly of the Portuguese King in West Africa and that of the Spanish King in Spanish America; yet some of his ventures were financially backed by high-ranking court officials, including Lord Admiral Clinton and Robert Dudley, while Elizabeth herself invested in the second voyage and tacitly approved the third. Greed was no doubt a powerful motive but as Pollitt has suggested 'aside from the profit motive there was a strong possibility that the trade was being used by the Crown as an instrument of its policies' (**107**, p. 39). The third voyage ended in disaster when Hawkins's ships were destroyed by the Spaniards in the harbour of San Juan de Ulloa, in September 1568 (**107**).

Another opportunity to harass the Spaniards arose in 1568 and it was this which led to the first major open quarrel with Spain. In November Spanish ships containing about 400,000 florins in cash took refuge from bad weather and Channel privateers in English ports. The money was a loan from Genoese bankers to be used to meet some of the cost of Alva's army in the Netherlands. Elizabeth at first seemed ready to provide a naval escort to protect the ships on their journey onwards. Then, when she learned from Cecil that the money legally still belonged to the Genoese bankers and was not yet Philip's, she decided to take over the loan herself. The view taken by some historians that this move was 'a pointless act of piracy' and 'as costly as it was senseless' cannot be sustained (**91**, p. 26). The evidence, limited as it is, suggests that the motive was to make life as difficult as possible for Alva in the Netherlands. For Cecil, the prime mover in the affair, what was at stake was not just the money but the security of England and the future of the whole protestant cause in Europe (**53**). The fate of Hawkins's third expedition may also have played a part in Cecil's decision to seize the treasure ships. On 3 December, William Hawkins heard the first rumours of his brother's losses at San Juan and, albeit mistakenly, of his brother's death. Immediately he passed on the news to Cecil, with the plea that Spanish goods be seized in reprisal, whilst at the same time informing him that the treasure then in English ports was not legally Spanish property. Cecil, disquieted to hear 'with what cruelty he [Hawkins] was used, under pretence of friendship' and armed with a legal justification for seizure, acted at once (**7**, **73**, p. 430). It seems likely that neither Cecil nor Elizabeth expected a violent reaction from the Spanish government. Seizures of ships on one pretext or another were common in the sixteenth century and the English government's actions were not indefensible in law. De Spes, however, panicked when he suspected what Elizabeth intended to do and urged Alva to seize English ships and property in the Netherlands even before Elizabeth's decision was announced [**doc. 16**]. This Alva did and immediately the English government retaliated in kind. Philip II also seized English ships and goods in Spanish ports. The result was a total suspension of Anglo-Spanish trade (**87**).

While the seizure had dramatic domestic repercussions, its effect on foreign policy was less significant. It initiated a diplomatic crisis and, in the short term, relations deteriorated between the two governments. For a time, Philip gave support to Elizabeth's enemies: he authorised Alva to encourage and give money to the Catholics of the North in 1569, though he drew back from committing himself to their cause when he realised their weakness; in 1571 he was enthusiastic about the Ridolfi plot and instructed the more cautious Alva to send 10,000 soldiers to England in support of the Catholics. Elizabeth too was more openly hostile to

Spain. English privateers co-operated with the Netherlands' Sea Beggars and Huguenots in attacking and looting Spanish ships. A marriage alliance with the Duke of Anjou was mooted and, when this failed, a treaty of friendship was signed with the French at Blois in 1572, whereby each promised the other aid when asked (**87**). Nevertheless, by 1572 both Philip and Elizabeth were ready to settle their differences and it was clear that the rupture of 1568 was not to be permanent. In 1573 a limited agreement for two years was reached (Convention of Nymegen) whereby trade was reopened. The next year, they signed the Convention of Bristol (**54**). This improvement in diplomatic relations caused the English government to withdraw its support from maritime ventures in the Spanish Indies. Elizabeth would not grant a licence to Richard Grenville to embark on a new voyage of discovery in 1574. The English raids which continued in the Indies were entirely private in character until 1577 and did not appear to be a cause of friction between the Spanish and English governments (**18**).

The prospects of a continuing accord between England and Spain were shattered by events in the Netherlands. In 1572, Elizabeth's expulsion of the privateering Sea Beggars from English ports resulted in their unexpected capture of Brill and in the reopening of the revolt of the Netherlands (**93**). Elizabeth's handling of the Netherlands crisis is a matter of some controversy. R. B. Wernham has argued that Elizabeth followed a consistent policy towards the Netherlands for the rest of her reign. It was, he writes, a policy built on fear of France as much as on fear of Spain. 'She wanted to retain Spain as a counterpoise to France. She wanted the Netherlands, though restored to their ancient liberties, to remain Spanish so that they would not become French' (**86**, p. 320). In this policy, Wernham concludes, she was both far-sighted and successful. Professor Wilson, on the other hand, has described Elizabeth's policy as 'a bewildering succession of expedients' (**91**, p. 16). He doubts her sincerity in calling for the restoration of the Netherlands' liberties; and although he accepts as genuine her fear of France, he considers it exaggerated and groundless. Finally he judges her policy to be a dismal failure. Her prevarications, he argues, drove the rebels into the arms of France in 1581, while her refusal to support Orange in 1577 hastened the divisions in the rebel ranks, for only her military support could have given him sufficient military stature to quell noble opposition to his power (**91**).

In a detailed study of Elizabeth's policy in the 1570s and 1580s

Professor MacCaffrey has presented both a more complex and more convincing view than either that of Wilson or Wernham. Unlike Wilson, he detects consistent principles in her foreign policy towards the Netherlands. On the negative side, she did not seek dynastic expansion and regularly turned down opportunities to acquire Continental lands as the price of her support for the rebels. Positively she was concerned with national defence: first, to prevent France expanding into the Netherlands and thereby controlling the coast from Brittany to Groningen; secondly, to persuade the Spanish government to accept a religious and political compromise which would include the removal of Spanish troops and a return to provincial autonomy. Yet, unlike Wernham, MacCaffrey sees Elizabeth at the mercy of events rather than the initiator of a consistent foreign policy, for while her principles remained constant, she was compelled to react in an *ad hoc* fashion to changes in the international situation over which she had little or no control. He demonstrates that Elizabeth's policy was 'largely reactive in nature, responding to the ebb and flow of events across the North Sea'. She was always ready to bend to the realities of events and to live 'from day to day . . . improvising as the situation demanded' (**54**, p. 193).

An analysis of Elizabeth's responses to events in the Netherlands demonstrates the validity of MacCaffrey's thesis. The three years following the rebel seizure of Brill seemed to offer little hope of an eventual Spanish defeat. Only two provinces, Holland and Zeeland, were in revolt, while the Spanish army was experienced and well commanded. Accordingly, despite both popular support in England for the rebels, as seen in the public celebrations of their capture of Middelburg in 1574, and pressure from the Prince of Orange and his influential supporters at Elizabeth's court (Leicester and Walsingham in particular), the Queen was determined to maintain a policy of 'ostentatious neutrality' and to offer herself as an impartial mediator. At times she did give hidden help to the rebels by allowing them to recruit English volunteers and to purchase supplies, whilst also preventing English mercenaries from entering Alva's service. Nevertheless, she consistently refused to give Orange official aid; there was little advantage in alienating Spain irrevocably on behalf of a small band of rebels who seemed destined ultimately to come to terms with Philip (**54**).

Only during the second half of 1575 did Elizabeth's policy begin to shift direction. In that summer the Spanish successfully launched a new military offensive. It looked as though either the Spanish

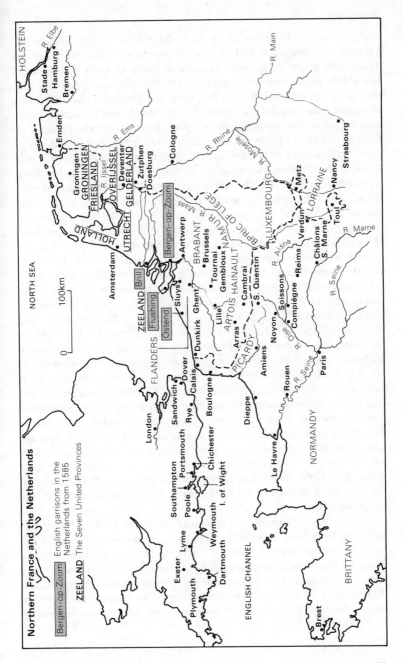

Northern France and the Netherlands

Bergen-op-Zoom — English garrisons in the Netherlands from 1585

ZEELAND — The Seven United Provinces

NORTH SEA

HOLSTEIN

R. Elbe

Stade
Hamburg
Bremen

Emden

R. Ems

Groningen
GRONINGEN
FRIESLAND
OVERIJSSEL
R. IJssel
GELDERLAND
Zutphen
Deventer
Doesburg
UTRECHT

Amsterdam
HOLLAND

Brill
ZEELAND
Flushing
Ostend
Sluys
FLANDERS
Ghent
Dunkirk
Lille

Antwerp
Bergen-op-Zoom
BRABANT
Brussels
Gembloux
Tournai
HAINAULT
Cambrai
S. Quentin
ARTOIS
Arras
PICARDY

Cologne

R. Rhine

R. Moselle

NAMUR R. Maas
BRIC OF LIÈGE
LUXEMBOURG

Metz
Verdun
LORRAINE
Nancy
Toul

Strasbourg

R. Main

London

Dover
Sandwich
Rye
Calais
Boulogne

Chichester
Portsmouth
Southampton
Poole
Weymouth
I. of Wight
Dartmouth
Lyme
Exeter
Plymouth

Dieppe
Le Havre
Rouen

Amiens
Noyon
Soissons
Compiègne
Reims
Châlons
S. Marne
Paris

R. Seine
R. Oise
R. Aisne
R. Marne
R. Seine

NORMANDY

BRITTANY

Brest

ENGLISH CHANNEL

0   100km

65

army would soon triumph or that the rebels would call in the French in a desperate bid to save themselves. Still determined to avoid aiding the rebels but anxious to forestall both possibilities, Elizabeth made new overtures to the Spanish government. She offered again to mediate; but this time, significantly, she laid down the terms she required as part of a reconciliation settlement: the restoration of the Netherlands' ancient liberties and the removal of foreign troops. On religion she was equivocal; probably she envisaged Catholicism as the official religion with the protestants being granted freedom of worship in private. Had these terms been accepted, the Netherlands would have returned to the political situation under Charles V, and this would have posed no security threat to England. By specifying conditions that she considered necessary for England's security, Elizabeth was stepping away from the position of neutrality carefully established since 1572 (**54**).

The events in the Netherlands during 1576 drove Elizabeth further along this route. The Spanish army's mutinies of that year, which culminated in the sack of Antwerp, terrorised the local population and pushed all seventeen provinces into open rebellion. An Estates-General* representing the whole Netherlands was summoned and in October drew up an agreement with Holland and Zeeland, known as the Pacification of Ghent. As the opposition to Spain was no longer confined to two provinces but extended to the whole of the Netherlands, the Estates appeared a more acceptable ally to Elizabeth. Furthermore the Pacification called for the expulsion of foreign troops and the restoration of the provinces' ancient liberties – the very terms sought by Elizabeth. As a result, Elizabeth promised the Estates a loan of £100,000 if the Spanish government refused to accept the Pacification. In fact, due to lack of money, the new Governor-General of the Netherlands, Don John, had little choice but to accept. In February 1577 he signed the so-called Perpetual Edict. In April the Spanish army left the Netherlands for Italy.

Elizabeth's diplomatic victory was short-lived. War broke out between Don John and the Estates in the summer of 1577 and the Spanish troops were recalled. There were also rumours that a French army would be sent to aid Don John, whilst Elizabeth's spy network discovered that Don John was plotting with Mary Stuart. The danger to England's security seemed to require drastic remedies. Accordingly Elizabeth promised the Estates an immediate £100,000 and offered them English troops if and when the French forces arrived. At the same time she warned Philip that if he did not accept the Pacification and recall Don John, she would give military aid to the rebels. In this policy Elizabeth had the full support of her Council (**61**).

Philip neither accepted the Pacification nor recalled Don John; yet Elizabeth did not send an English army to the Netherlands. Why not? First, the response of the Estates to her offer had been less than satisfactory. They had shown reluctance to accept English soldiers and, without informing Elizabeth, had invited Archduke Matthias to act as their governor. Secondly, the factionalism developing amongst the Estates, and the military weakness they displayed at the battle of Gembloux in January 1578 against the army of Don John, made them appear unreliable allies. Thirdly, Elizabeth's Council, so recently united, began to offer conflicting advice. Leicester and Walsingham continued to press for intervention, but Sussex, for one, pointed to the danger of entering a war against Spain. Elizabeth listened to the voices of caution and drew back from open intervention (**54, 119**) [**doc. 19** (a) and (b)].

Nevertheless Elizabeth could not afford to leave the Estates to their fate, for it might mean their total submission to the military power of Spain or their rescue by ambitious leaders in France. As Sussex wrote, 'the case wylbe harde bothe with the Queen and with Ingland yf ether the Frenche possesse or the Spanyardes tyranyse in the Low Contryes' (**119**, p. 353). After another unsuccessful attempt to mediate, she decided in April 1578 to hire John Casimir of the Palatinate to fight for the Estates with 11,000 mercenaries. Before Casimir's arrival in the Netherlands, however, Francis, Duke of Anjou, the French King's brother, entered Hainault to aid the rebels. In August the Estates granted him the title 'Defender of the Liberties of the Low Countries'. Casimir arrived soon afterwards; but instead of leading a united Estates-General against the Spaniards, he became involved in aiding the radical Calvinists against the Catholic Malcontents*, thus intensifying the religious tensions amongst the Netherlands' rebels (**62**).

By the end of 1578 Elizabeth's foreign policy in response to the Netherlands' crisis was in disarray. The Spanish government had consistently rejected her offers of mediation and was deeply suspicious of her intentions. The rebels, enfeebled by religious, political and personal differences, looked unable to hold their own against the Spaniards. Anjou was embarking on a military adventure in the Netherlands which might result in French territorial gains. Elizabeth had managed to alienate the Spaniards without aiding the Dutch or keeping out the French. It is difficult to understand how

Professor Wernham could include this period of her foreign policy in a chapter entitled 'High water mark' (**86**). The marriage negotiation which Elizabeth opened with Anjou in 1579 was a desperate attempt to improve the situation. At best Elizabeth hoped that, if the marriage took place, pressure by France and England on Philip would lead to a settlement in the Netherlands along the lines of the Pacification of Ghent. At the very least she saw the marriage as a means by which she could control Anjou if he continued with his schemes there. In the event the marriage negotiations came to nothing; but the personal contact which Elizabeth had with Anjou during their course alleviated her fears about his character and ambitions to such an extent that she was now prepared to sponsor his expedition to the Netherlands (**62, 103**).

But it was not only her confidence in Anjou which brought about this new direction in foreign policy. The dramatic growth of Spanish power between 1579 and 1581 had convinced her that Anglo-French co-operation was required 'to impeach the King of Spain's greatness' (**10**, p. 353). In 1580, Philip II invaded Portugal and the following year was recognised as King by the Portuguese *Cortes**. At a stroke he had acquired another rich colonial empire and also a substantial fleet which gave him the resources to mount a seaborne invasion of England; his designs on England seemed confirmed by Spanish support for two Papal expeditions to Ireland in 1579 and 1580. On the Netherlands front, the policy of Alexander Farnese, Prince of Parma, the new Governor-General, was transforming the military and political situation to the advantage of Spain. By 1581 he had reached agreements with the South Walloon provinces (southern Flanders, Artois and Hainault) and the Catholic Stadtholder* of the north-eastern provinces, and was ready to begin his reconquest of the north.

Elizabeth, consequently, pursued more openly anti-Spanish policies. Not only did she subsidise Anjou, but she proposed an Anglo-French league against Spain in 1581. She welcomed Don Antonio, the pretender to the Portuguese throne, at court and contemplated sending a force to the Azores on his behalf. The same year, amid public celebration, she knighted Francis Drake for his maritime exploits against the Spaniards. Anti-Spanish sentiment was so strong that the Spanish ambassador was either ignored or treated with contempt at court (**54, 86, 87**). On the whole, Elizabeth's policy was unsuccessful. Henry III of France would not assume an anti-Spanish stance, while Anjou in the Netherlands proved a disaster. Philip II tightened his grip on Portugal by completing the occupation of the Azores in 1583, and Parma won victory after victory in Flanders and Brabant. The deaths of William of Orange and Anjou in 1584 seemed to remove the last obstacles to the restoration of Spanish power in the Netherlands and the consequent invasion of England (**62**). The death of Anjou had other important repercussions. It left the protestant Henry of Navarre as heir presumptive to the throne of France and so opened the final phase in the French religious struggles. To prevent Navarre's eventual succession, the Catholic League and the Guises concluded in secret the Treaty of Joinville (December 1584) with Philip II by which he promised the Guises his protection and subsidies. The danger to Elizabeth was acute. In the first place, with the Guises in his pocket, Philip looked upon the claims of Mary Stuart with more favour. Secondly, there was no longer the power of France to check the overmighty Spain (**54, 86**). Even before the Treaty of Joinville was made known to Elizabeth, she had hoped to persuade Henry III to take up the role of protector of the Dutch. In February 1585, however, Henry had turned down the offer and thrown the responsibility for aiding the rebels back on England. In the following month Elizabeth heard rumours of the treaty, which exposed the threat to England's security. In May, Philip ordered the seizure of English shipping in Spanish ports. Although he probably had not made a final decision to invade England, but rather was hoping to undermine England's strength by disrupting Anglo-Spanish trade, Elizabeth and her councillors assumed that the ships were seized to augment an invasion fleet. Furthermore, those merchants who had been benefiting most from Anglo-Iberian trade and whose attitude to Spain had consequently been ambivalent, at once clamoured for the right of reprisal; the economic arguments in favour of continued peace were forgotten (**17**).

In these circumstances, Elizabeth listened favourably in June 1585 to a Dutch embassy which offered her their sovereignty and pleaded for regular military aid. Though she refused to accept sovereignty, she signed the Treaty of Nonsuch which committed her to pay for 5000 foot and 1000 horse to be sent to the Netherlands under an English commander. As security for her support and repayment of her expenses she was given control of the towns of Brill and Flushing. At the same time she sent Drake to release the English ships in Spain and raid the ports and shipping of the Caribbean. Despite these provocative actions, Elizabeth still hoped for peace. No sooner had she signed the Nonsuch treaty than she began to extend unofficial peace-feelers to Parma and to reconsider her decision to send troops. Leicester, her chosen commander, sighed with relief when he was at last allowed to go, for 'no man hath had more discouragements' (**54**, p. 352; **2**). Similarly Elizabeth hesitated to unleash Drake and his fleet till the very last moment. No wonder that when the order to leave finally came, the fleet set sail in some disarray, fearing the order would be revoked, for 'we [were] not the most assured of Her Majesty's perseverance to let us go forward' (**18**, p. 98).

France 1564–85

In 1564 Elizabeth signed the Peace of Troyes which ended hostilities with France. Thereafter she preferred to remain a bystander to the spectacle of seemingly endless civil wars in France. No longer did she try to exploit French weakness and recapture Calais. War was too expensive and risky, especially as the Huguenots had demonstrated their unreliability as allies in 1563. Unmoved by pleas that they were protestant brethren in need of her protection, Elizabeth appeared more influenced by the fact that, despite their princely titles, the Huguenots were rebels against their lawful sovereign. Nevertheless, Elizabeth could not afford to be an impartial observer. If the Guises were to secure control of France, her throne and England's security would be under threat. Consequently, she acted on several fronts whenever that danger seemed imminent.

Primarily, Elizabeth tried to co-operate with Catherine de Medici who, by following a policy of peace at home and abroad, was the main political counterweight to the Guises. With this in mind, Elizabeth pressed ahead with the marriage negotiations between Anjou and herself in 1570–71, insincere though her commitment to such a marriage was. In 1572 she signed the Treaty of Blois, partly to strengthen Catherine, partly to bind her in a defensive alliance against Spain. Even after the massacre of St Bartholomew, Elizabeth did not break off relations with the French court, although relations distinctly cooled (**79, 80**).

Catherine, however, was not always in control of royal policymaking. When the Catholic faction seemed to be dominant at the French court, Elizabeth had to resort to giving aid to the Huguenots in order to ensure their political and military survival. They were granted unofficial help in 1568, through an arrangement whereby the Huguenots at La Rochelle would exchange some of their products for munitions from the English Merchant Adventurers. In 1570 Elizabeth went one stage further and made formal offers of money; three years later she agreed to send secret supplies of munitions to La Rochelle. From 1585 she subsidised Henry of Navarre (**73, 74**). When the danger from the Guises seemed most acute, Elizabeth even considered direct intervention in the French civil wars. In September 1568 she was informed that the Guises were planning to launch an attack on the Huguenot leaders as a preliminary to arranging a marriage between Anjou and Mary Stuart and invading England, possibly with Spanish help. In response, her ambassador told the French court that she would intervene because of 'the duty to her subjects, the friendship she has for the King and the preservation of her own estate' – a message clearly intended as a warning to the Cardinal of Lorraine (**79**, pp. 168–69). In 1575 Elizabeth went much further. With the death of Charles IX the previous year, his brother Henry of Anjou succeeded to the throne. Henry was known in England as a fanatical Catholic and close associate of the Guises. Consequently, when a broad-based coalition of Huguenots, *Politiques** and princes of the blood asked Elizabeth to back their bid for power, she agreed, and had not this opposition group been reconciled with Henry III at the Peace of Monsieur, in 1576, she might well have been drawn into the civil wars (**54**).

The Guise threat not only made Elizabeth take an active interest in French politics, but involved her too in the affairs of Scotland. From 1560 to 1568, French influence in Scotland was at a low point. The success of the 1560 expedition and the eclipse of Guise power in France helped loosen the links between the two realms. Catherine de Medici was unsympathetic to Mary Stuart; she opposed any suggestion of a marriage between Mary and Anjou and after Mary's defeat by her subjects at the battle of Carberry Hill in 1567 she recommended that the Queen be confined to a convent. The Guises, however, had other plans for their kinswoman, and the political instability in Scotland after 1570 gave them the opportunities to try and realise them (**32, 79, 80**).

The assassination of Regent Moray in January 1570 plunged Scotland into a civil war between the Marians and the adherents of the young King James. The Marians looked to the Guises for military aid whilst the supporters of James sought help from Elizabeth. Yet Elizabeth did not want to send military aid to the protestant King's party for several reasons. First, Elizabeth could not afford a confrontation with France in the aftermath of the Northern Rebellion and at a time when she was quarrelling with Spain.

Secondly, she was still considering whether or not to restore Mary and hence thought it unwise to strengthen the Scottish Queen's opponents. On the other hand, under pressure from her Council, she realised that some action was required. 'The Frenche wyll shortely have a grette factyon ther than wylbe fer our proffyte her,' wrote Sussex, who was her President of the Council of the North (**119**, p. 274). Even worse, the Marians had joined up with fugitive rebels from the 1569 rising and were mounting a series of raids on the English side of the border. Fearing that these were but a preliminary to a full-scale Franco-Scottish invasion, Elizabeth ordered an army into Scotland with the limited purpose of destroying the power of the Scottish border lords and flushing out the English rebels. Accordingly, in April, Sussex raided the Scottish borders, devastated the dales and seized the principal strongholds (**119**).

However, the military success of the raid was short-lived and it failed completely in its purpose. The English rebels, still in conjunction with their Scottish allies, soon resumed their attacks on the English borders. The King's party remained weak and in disarray; 'the sone's partie daily decayeth, the mother's partie daily increaseth,' wrote Sussex (**119**, p. 282). The French continued to pose a threat. Just before the raid, there were rumours that a French force was preparing to go to Dumbarton Castle, held by the Marians; immediately afterwards Charles IX demanded the withdrawal of the English troops and announced that if Elizabeth assisted the King's party he would help the Marians (**119**).

Elizabeth was still unwilling to give direct aid to the Scottish protestants but Sussex did not share his Queen's reluctance [**doc. 17**]. On his own initiative, taking advantage of her instructions 'to comforte our party there' and to negotiate a truce, he openly encouraged the King's supporters and offered military support if they assisted him in suppressing the English rebels. As the Marians would not surrender the rebels, he sent troops to Edinburgh in May to join with the protestant lords assembled there and harass the Marian lords. The Queen approved this venture as its ostensible aim was to frighten the Marians into giving up the rebels. However, when the French informed her that there would ensue a 'kind of war' between England and France if she continued to attack the Marians, Elizabeth immediately ordered the withdrawal of her forces and opened discussions for the restoration of Mary. In response Charles IX revoked his order to send troops to Scotland (**119**).

All was quiet for a couple of months. In July, however, the Marians once more challenged the King's party, threatened to call in the French, and resumed their protection of the English rebels who again raided the English borders. Pressed by Sussex to act, Elizabeth agreed to a third incursion across the frontier. To safeguard her negotiations with Mary and to forestall French threats, Elizabeth insisted that Sussex should make his raid look punitive. Nevertheless she told him that if the limited raid did not bring security to the King's supporters 'we do warrant you to give them ayde of some part of our army' (**119**, p. 307). This third expedition was the most successful politically. The border lords submitted to Elizabeth and abandoned the rebels, many of whom left Scotland. There was no need for Sussex to use his troops against the Marians, as they too surrendered and agreed to disarm. The French did not intervene (**119**).

After this success, Elizabeth tried to withdraw from military involvement in Scotland. She preferred to continue negotiations for the restoration of Mary and to reach a rapprochment with France. The Ridolfi plot put an end to her hopes for the former, but the latter was achieved thanks to the return of Catherine de Medici to power after the third war of religion. Nevertheless, the possibility of a revival of French influence in Scotland remained and was still a matter of concern to Elizabeth's Council. As Burghley pointed out, France could not afford to abandon the Marians and so an Anglophile regent for Scotland was urgently needed to restore order and keep out the French. For this purpose, Elizabeth sent her troops again into Scotland, in November 1572, to capture Edinburgh Castle and thereby to help the pro-English regent, Morton. Once Morton had asserted political control, Elizabeth withdrew from giving further support to his régime for fear that France would break off the *entente* achieved at Blois. She would neither enter a protestant league with Morton nor even grant pensions to the Scottish lords to ensure their continued loyalty (**74, 86**).

Morton dominated Scottish politics, with England's diplomatic support, until 1579. In that year James's cousin Esmé Stuart, Sieur d'Aubigny arrived in Scotland, won James's favour and engineered Morton's fall and execution (1580–81). These developments alarmed the English government, for Stuart was believed to be a Guise agent working to persuade James to renounce his protestantism, marry a French princess and claim the English throne. Yet despite advice from councillors such as Leicester and Walsingham, Elizabeth would not intervene to save Morton or destroy Stuart.

She was afraid that military pressure from England would push the Scots into the arms of the French, as Morton had little support amongst his own nobility, and that it might lead the French to halt the negotiations she had just initiated for a league against Spain. While Elizabeth waited upon events, Stuart was bringing about his own downfall by quarrelling with the Scottish presbyterian leaders. In August 1582 a group of protestant lords kidnapped the King in the Ruthven raid and detained Stuart. English agents had paid money over to the conspirators but it is unknown how far Elizabeth's government was implicated in the plot. Stuart, in fear of his life, fled to France but the French were powerless to help him. Elizabeth still needed to wean James from an independent or pro-French position. This she could not manage until 1586 when the size of the pension James was to receive from her was eventually agreed upon (**54, 74**).

Thus Elizabeth, after 1560, consistently demonstrated a marked reluctance to give financial or military aid to the protestant pro-English party in Scotland. Only extreme pressure from her Council or men on the spot could induce her to give it limited support in 1570, 1571 and 1572. These were times when the threat of French intervention seemed to be greatest. Unlike most of her Tudor predecessors, Elizabeth demonstrated little or no interest in absorbing Scotland into England; perhaps she was aware that the task would be done for her through the succession of James to the English throne.

While it was the Guises and Catholic faction which favoured a forward policy in Scotland, it was their opponents who pursued a policy of military intervention in the Netherlands. There had been secret contacts between the leaders of the French Huguenots and the Netherlands' opposition to Philip II from as early as 1566. In 1568 some 3000 Huguenots invaded Artois to aid the Prince of Orange, whilst in 1572 the Huguenot leader, Admiral Coligny, persuaded Charles IX to order a French army into Flanders (**61**). Zealots like Walsingham and Leicester regarded the prospect of a protestant league against Spain with enthusiasm and hoped for English participation. Elizabeth and councillors like Burghley and Sussex, on the other hand, viewed the prospect with alarm. They feared French ambitions and believed that a French presence in the Netherlands would be even more dangerous to England's security than the Spanish one. If the French occupied Flanders they would control the coast from Brittany to Antwerp, threaten English trade and challenge English sovereignty on the narrow seas. Without the communications problems of the Spaniards, the French would moreover be less vulnerable to internal opposition or external attack. A memorandum of Burghley best, expressed this viewpoint [**doc. 18**]. Although Burghley was sympathetic to the Dutch rebels, he recommended at this point (June 1572) that if the Spaniards were incapable of keeping the French out of the Netherlands, the Queen should, given certain conditions, intervene on their side against the French. These precautions were in the event unnecessary, for French aid to the rebels came to nothing. A small French force of 6000 was wiped out by the Spaniards in July 1572, and the massacre of St Bartholomew in August prevented further French involvement for some years (**86**).

As Orange was convinced of the urgent need for foreign assistance against Spain, and as English aid was not forthcoming, the rebels appealed once more to the French. It was not until 1578 that they received a positive response. Francis, Duke of Anjou (known as Alençon until 1578), agreed to sent troops. To meet the danger Elizabeth veered towards a well-worn diplomatic manoeuvre. Once she had satisfied herself that Anjou was acting independently of the French government, she decided to woo him into her camp. A marriage, she hoped, would give her the means to control the Duke and to put effective pressure on Philip to make a negotiated peace close to the terms of the Pacification of Ghent. In this policy she had the support of only one or two of her councillors; Sussex definitely [**doc. 20a**] and Burghley probably. The others were firmly opposed to it. Elizabeth, nevertheless, pressed on with the marriage negotiations from the spring of 1578 until the end of 1579. For the first time, it seems, Elizabeth herself was ready to marry, and for personal as well as political reasons. Only when she faced manifestations of popular hostility to the match and the obvious reluctance of her Council to accept it, did she back down (**103**) [**doc. 20b**]. By that time, Elizabeth's fears of Spanish power were overtaking her mistrust of French ambitions. Consequently, once she had discarded the idea of marriage as politically impossible, she was ready to negotiate an Anglo-French league against Spain. In July 1581, she sent Walsingham to Paris to offer secret aid for an Anjou expedition to the Netherlands and to propose an Anglo-French league. It was a new direction in Elizabethan foreign policy and was a reaction to the dramatic growth in Spanish power in the years 1579–81. Henry III, however, was unconvinced that Spanish victories constituted a threat to France's security. Nor was he convinced that Elizabeth was sincere in her offers of aid or a league.

As Walsingham reported, Henry feared to commit himself to military action against Spain 'lest when he should be imbarqued, your Majestie would slip the collar' (**10**, p. 361). Only if Elizabeth were to marry Anjou, as a token of her good faith, would Henry agree to enter a league. This Elizabeth could not do because of domestic policy considerations. Her past record of prevarications, half-promises and *volte faces* had caught up with her at a critical time.

Although she secured neither the marriage nor the league, Elizabeth none the less decided to back Anjou's expedition in the Netherlands. In August 1581, hearing that Henry had refused to provide Anjou with funds, she decided to step into the breach. She could not watch passively while the Spaniards reconquered the Netherlands yet she was still not prepared to send English troops there for fear that it would involve her in a lone war against Spain. Anjou had won her confidence, and she believed she could control him. Consequently she gave him subsidies (£60,000 in 1581–82) and her sponsorship (**54, 74**). Anjou, however, was the wrong man for the job. His expedition ended in disaster with an abortive attempt to seize Antwerp, which resulted in the loss of half his men. He returned to France in June 1583 and died there the following year. On his death, Elizabeth tried to persuade the French King to take on his mantle and aid the Dutch rebels against Spain. As Walsingham wrote, Elizabeth was 'now so convinced of Spanish bad will that she preferred the risks of French domination to Spanish restoration' (**54**, p. 307). Henry III, however, confronted by the Catholic League at home, was in no position to aid Calvinist rebels against Spain, and Elizabeth ultimately had to act alone.

War 1585–1603

No formal declaration of war was made against Spain in 1585, but the Leicester expedition to the Netherlands and Drake's raids in Spain and the West Indies were acts of open warfare. Elizabeth, however, viewed the war as a form of politics by other means, an intensification of diplomatic pressure to convince Philip that England was too powerful either to invade or to ignore. Consequently, she intended her intervention to be as limited as possible. At sea she preferred to rely heavily on the initiative of private sailors and shipowners rather than send a royal navy in force against the Spaniards. On land, she viewed her troops as merely a relief expedition to halt the inexorable progress of Parma and was consequently furious when Leicester, in January 1586, accepted the title of Governor-General (**18, 54**) [**doc. 21**].

Philip II viewed Elizabeth's actions in a different light. They strengthened, rather than deterred, his resolve to attack England directly. Drake's voyages had not severely damaged the Spanish economy. His fleet had missed the Spanish treasure ships and had seized booty worth only about £60,000, whilst Spanish commerce reached a peak in 1585–86. Yet the raids had exposed the vulnerability of Spain's colonial defences and injured her prestige. Leicester's expedition had likewise resulted in no major victory for the rebels. Although his troops recaptured Zutphen and Doesburg (August 1586) and thus secured the Ijssel crossings, Deventer and Zutphen were betrayed to Parma by their English Catholic officers in January 1587, and, in July, Sluys was captured by the Spaniards. Furthermore Leicester's political manoeuvres served merely to intensify the regional, factional and religious splits within the rebel ranks which weakened the Dutch ability to fight (**2, 61, 62**). Yet the very presence of English troops in the Netherlands seemed, at least at first, to help Dutch morale. Philip and Parma both believed that without the arrival of Leicester the rebels would have sought a negotiated settlement. They were thus convinced that the reconquest of the Netherlands could only be achieved once English help was withdrawn. Throughout 1586 and early 1587 plans were formed for the 'Enterprise of England'. Men and munitions were amassed in the summer of 1587; all was ready for an invasion that year. Drake's 1587 expedition to Cadiz could only postpone the campaign for a year (**18, 56, 61, 62**).

The Armada was designed to clear the Channel so that Parma's troops could land from the Netherlands. At best, Philip hoped the invasion would encourage the English Catholics to rise, overthrow Elizabeth and welcome a pro-Spanish government. But the more probable outcome, he envisaged, was that Parma would land, occupy Kent (and perhaps London too) and then use these territorial gains to negotiate a favourable settlement which would leave the Dutch isolated (**63**). The mere threat of the Spanish Armada had secured advantages for Spain. In February 1587 Elizabeth began informal peace discussions with Parma, whilst the Estates, suspicious of her intentions, halted their co-operation with the English forces. They also refused to send ships to help to defend England in June 1588. Yet this was not sufficient for Philip II; in the belief that God was on his side, he risked his fleet in war, determined to defeat England the first stage in the suppression of the Netherlands (**62**).

The Spanish defeat owed much to the work of John Hawkins at the navy from 1577, but the winds and geography played an important part in turning a military setback into a major disaster (**57**). The defeat of the Spanish Armada rescued the Dutch and saved England but it did not end the war. In fact the war was extended, as Elizabeth agreed to offensive operations in France, Portugal and the Atlantic. Her handling of overall strategy has been criticised by both contemporaries and some historians. The failure of the 'silver blockade', the debacle of the Rouen expedition and the fiasco of the Portugal campaign in 1589 have all been cited as evidence of Elizabeth's weaknesses as a war commander. Yet such criticisms are misplaced, for they arise from a misunder-standing of Elizabeth's intentions and an underestimation of her difficulties (**115**).

Elizabeth's principal war aims against Spain, unlike those of many of her commanders and advisers, were neither the destruction of Spanish power nor the acquisition of a colonial empire. In war as in peace she sought, above all, national security. In practical terms, this meant a favourable settlement in the Netherlands, the freedom of the French Channel ports from Spanish control, and the survival of Spain and France as strong independent powers. Consequently, she had no conception of an overall grand strategy to bring Spain to its knees; she did not seriously contemplate an invasion of Spain or Portugal, a full-scale silver blockade, or the seizure of colonial bases. At sea, she sought to use the English fleets merely to disrupt Spanish communications, intercept Spanish treasure and defend home waters. On land, she was prepared to send armies only to make limited strikes to attain limited objectives, as when she reinforced Henry of Navarre's campaign against the Guises and the Spanish army (**17, 52, 87, 115**).

Elizabeth's modest wartime objectives were partly the result of foreign policy considerations (the need to retain a powerful Spain to check the power of France) and partly due to her recognition of the limited military resources at her disposal. Elizabeth did not allow her parsimony to dictate her policies to the extent that she did everything by halves; for her campaigns in France in 1589–92 she raised levies to recruit new men and continually overspent her budgets. She was only too well aware, however, of the limitations of her purse and the unpopularity of her expedients to raise necessary sums, and she cut her royal cloak accordingly. She insisted that her allies should pay their share of the cost of campaigns, and she avoided ambitious ventures (**52**). The decision to pursue a privateering war rather than to attack the Spanish navy can be seen in the same light. Dependent as she was on private enterprise for her fleets, she had to allow her captains and investors to pursue the type of warfare that would bring them profit as well as strengthen national security (**17, 87**).

The Queen's inadequate resources affected the success of her policies as well as their scope. Dr Lloyd's *The Rouen Campaign 1590–92* amply illustrates how the raising, equipping and transporting of Essex's army soon revealed England's constrained official military capacity and disclosed the risks Elizabeth would run if she tested it too far. She was, therefore, forced to depend on allies whose aims were at variance with hers and with whom communications were difficult and slow (**52**) [**doc. 22**]. Similarly, the 1589 Portugal campaign failed because of organisational weaknesses and a serious confusion of aims. These were not the result of personal differences but the corollary of the joint-stock nature of the whole enterprise. Elizabeth herself primarily intended her fleet to destroy the remnants of the Armada harboured in Biscay ports. It was then to sail to the Azores to intercept the Spanish silver ships (**87, 115**). But she was reliant on private captains and investors with more grandiose and greedy aims who disobeyed her instructions and, in the Queen's words, 'went to places more for profit than for service' (**122**, p. 114). The result was a fiasco: the Armada fleet was left to be re-equipped, Drake never arrived at the Azores and there was great loss of English lives. Even worse, the whole expedition cost £100,000.

Ultimately Elizabeth's objectives were achieved. Spain was bloodied but undefeated. The Southern Netherlands were restored to Spain on a semi-autonomous basis while the Northern provinces remained free. France emerged from the civil wars with a monarch sufficiently strong to resist both Spain and the most fanatic French Catholics. Protestantism and national independence were safeguarded from foreign threats. Her policies did not achieve all this by themselves; external factors were more important, but the policies undoubtedly helped. From 1595 Elizabeth began to withdraw from the land war; military withdrawal from France was total while only a reduced number of troops remained in the Netherlands' cautionary towns. But the sea war continued until after Elizabeth's death. There were two more Spanish armadas and unsuccessful English expeditions to the Spanish Main and Caribbean. The war spread to Ireland where the Spaniards encouraged rebels and at one point tied down 17,000 English troops (**122**).

The cost of Elizabeth's success was high. The administrative machinery creaked under the strain of warfare. Anglo-Hispanic trade ground to a halt. The resulting economic and social grievances bred 'a new and more critical attitude to the central government, to the monarchy itself, and even to the monarch personally' (**75; 78; 87**, p. 92).

Part Three: Assessment

Foreign policy is more discernible to historians than it was to contemporaries. Reading through the day-to-day ambassadors' reports and Privy Council deliberations on relations with European states, it is easy to be overwhelmed by the amount of seeming trivia which absorbed the time and attention of Tudor governments. Maritime disputes, diplomatic protocol and trading conditions for merchants abroad were but some of the routine business which fill the pages of surviving records. Foreign policy was not a rational working out of political or strategic principles but instead a reaction to the immediate pressure of events, large and small, and it is worth remembering that governments could not always know when a circumstance was significant or when of little importance. Nevertheless, responses to events were not merely *ad hoc* with no reference to underlying goals. The question to be considered here is whether or not consistent goals emerged during the Tudor period. P. S. Crowson argues that Tudor foreign policy was based on three objectives: national defence, the maintenance of dynasty and the pursuit of economic advantage (**26**). This analysis, however, is superficial. Of course, all Tudor governments were sensitive to the problem of national security – as indeed governments have been before and since – but their perception of and responses to the problem differed widely. For example, the early Tudors, unlike Elizabeth, tended to equate national with dynastic security. Both Henry VIII and Mary, in order to secure the succession, promoted royal marriages which might have resulted in the loss of England's independence by making it the outlying possession of a foreign king. Furthermore, while Elizabeth viewed with increasing anxiety the prospect of hegemony in Europe by any power, Henry VIII had no such fears. Elizabeth after 1570 tried to ally with France to check the might of Spain, whereas in the 1520s and 1540s Henry had chosen to ally with Charles V, the strongest ruler in Europe, against France, the only power capable of resisting him.

As Crowson states, dynastic security and the pursuit of dynastic claims were certainly of prime importance in the Tudor period.

Henry VII frequently participated in European affairs to protect his dynasty against a usurper, and Henry VIII entered European wars to assert his dynastic claims to France. Elizabeth, on the other hand, was less influenced by dynastic considerations than her predecessors. After 1563 she effectively abandoned her dynastic claims to Calais, and in the late 1580s she did not try to recover the town as the price of her support to Henry of Navarre. Unlike Mary she did not seek a foreign marriage to produce a direct heir. The marriage negotiations with the Archduke may have been seriously pursued by her ambassador, Sussex, but Elizabeth herself placed every obstacle in the way of their successful outcome (**119**). The Alençon marriage scheme was not desired for dynastic reasons, since Elizabeth was probably too old to bear a child by 1579. Even Elizabeth's relations with Mary Stuart and their impact on foreign policy owed little to dynastic concerns. Mary's claim to the throne threatened England's religion and independence rather than the Tudor dynasty, for Elizabeth's spinsterhood had already condemned the line to extinction.

The pursuit of economic advantage was, as Crowson admits, a subsidiary aim of the Tudor monarchs. It was, moreover, viewed with varying degrees of enthusiasm by different governments. Henry VII was more interested than his son in finding new trade routes and extending overseas trade. Henry VIII was, indeed, indifferent to trading ventures beyond Europe, while Mary positively discouraged them and Elizabeth's attitude depended on the temperature of her political relations with Spain.

If the objectives of foreign policy did not remain constant during the Tudor period, can any consistent evolutionary development of policy be detected? R. B. Wernham concludes in his book, *Before the Armada* (**86**), that a pattern can be seen whereby England developed from a continental to a maritime power. At the beginning of Henry VII's reign, he argues, England had to come to terms with the loss of her Continental empire and with it her traditional role in European affairs. By 1588, England had adapted to the new situation and found herself a new role: expansion across the Atlantic, maritime ascendancy, and a defensive stance based on control of the Channel and opposition to the hegemony in Europe of any one power. This development, he asserts, was consciously brought about by the Tudor monarchs who gradually recognised and responded to the change in England's circumstances. Wernham appreciates that there were cross-currents, such as dynastic considerations, religious concerns and nostalgia for

European conquests. Nevertheless, he believes that there still can be discerned a clear picture of a developing policy. However, it is questionable whether this redirection of foreign policy was as conscious at the time as it now seems with hindsight. Tudor monarchs were both slow and reluctant to give up their territorial ambitions in Europe. The lure of the Hundred Years' War continued until well into Elizabeth's reign. Furthermore the outlook of Tudor governments remained firmly Continental even at the end of the period; their eyes were directed on Italy, Cleves and the Netherlands more than on the Caribbean or Africa. As Wernham himself points out in a later work, 'the Elizabethan war against Spain was first and foremost a continental European War . . . . It involved the whole of western Europe as well as, indeed more than, the Atlantic and Caribbean' (**122**, p. vii). Moreover, royal patronage of oceanic explorations was not consistent nor was the navy developed systematically and continuously; rather it was built up in fits and starts.

Tudor foreign policy is best considered as a series of discontinuities rather than as one coherent and developing theme. Radical changes of direction took place several times: on the accession of Henry VIII, for the duration of the 1530s, briefly in the early 1550s and then again in the late 1560s. Foreign policy under Elizabeth (after the early years of her reign) marks the clearest break with the past. She and her ministers thereafter put national interests before dynastic glory. In doing so, they were conscious of the danger from Spain, instead of being blinded by traditional hostility to France. Their perception of national interests, particularly security but also economic and religious interests, made Elizabethan foreign policy visionary, despite its many shortcomings, and gave it a quality of greatness. It also pointed the way to the future (though not in any clear line of progress), for, as Wernham writes, 'Elizabeth's government, like later English governments all through the succeeding centuries, could not view without very great alarm such a domination of Western Europe by a single over-mighty power' (**122**, p. 24).

Part Four: Documents

document 1
The cloth staple at Antwerp

This memorandum was written by Sir William Cecil, probably in 1564, at the time of strained relations between England and the Netherlands' government which resulted in an embargo on the cloth trade.

REASONS TO MOVE A FORBEARING OF THE RESTITUTION OF
THE INTERCOURSE TO ANTWERP

It is to be confessed of all men that it were better for this realm, for many considerations, that the commodities of the same were issued out rather to sundry places than to one, and specially to such one as the lord thereof is of so great power, as he may therewith annoy this realm by way of a war.

Secondly, it is probable that by the carrying over to Antwerp of such quantity of commodities out of the realm, as of late years is used, the shortness of the return multiplieth many merchants, and so consequently also this realm is overburdened with unnecessary foreign wares. And if the trade thereof should continue but a while, a great part of the treasure of the money of the realm would be carried thither to answer for such unnecessary trifles . . . .

Thirdly, it is to be thought that the diminution of clothing in this realm were profitable to the same for many causes. First, for that thereby the tillage of the realm is notoriously decayed, which is yearly manifest in that, contrary to former times, the realm is driven to be furnished with foreign corn, and specially the City of London. Secondly, for that the people that depend upon the making of cloth are of worse condition to be quietly governed than the husband men. Thirdly, by converting of so many people to clothing, the realm lacketh not only artificers, which were wont to inhabit all corporate towns, but also labourers for all common works.

Whereupon it followeth probably that it were profitable for the realm to have some alteration of the great trade of carrying of clothes out of the realm to Antwerp.

From Public Record Office State Papers, SP 12/35/38

document 2
Conflict with Spain over English trading and privateering expeditions

(a) *The King of Spain opposed English explorations and trading ventures which threatened the Spanish or Portuguese monopolies. Here John Mason, the English ambassador in Spain, was informing Queen Mary's Council of Philip II's hard-line attitude to English voyages to Guinea. The letter is dated 17 December 1553.*

I have thought good to signify unto your Lordships that his Majesty thinketh and then thought that oute of doubt that navigation was not be permitted, being the region plainely known to be in th'occupation of the King of Portugal, so as the said navigation might not be maintained without such notable inconvenience as were not expedient to be adventured; and yet being desirous to have our merchants helped as much as with reason they might be, he would travail that the said King of Portugal should take the merchandises by them provided at reasonable prices, which thing I did not then understand to be so far forth as his Majesty had taken order to have it to be put in execution, and therefore took I it not that overture to be a matter utterly resolved, upon which since then I have perceived to be otherwise. His gentle and courteous talk in this case and the declaration with many words of his displeasure that our merchants should by any mean be hindered, caused me somewhat to mistake his meaning and made me to write less peremptorely then I do now perceive his Majesty pleasure was I then should have done, and is that I shall now do, which is that as without injury the saide navigation cannot be continued, so taketh he the condition offered to the merchants to be the best way to save them as much harmless as may be, the quality of the case considered, which he thought your Lordships and the merchants would like accordingly, whereof his Majesty would gladly hear.

From Kervyn de Lettenhove, *Relations politiques des Pays-Bas et L'Angleterre*. Brussels, 1891, vol. 1, p. 11

(b) *The voyages of John Hawkins and Francis Drake particularly aroused the anger of the Spaniards. This report, dated Seville, 7 December 1569, demonstrates that some contemporary observers from overseas believed that Elizabeth was supporting the sailors for her own ends.*

From Cadiz this morning came the following news and immediately after it Don Melendez. He relates how John Hawkins the Englishman, who in New Spain last year had such a fight with the Viceroy and Don Francesco de Luxan, General of the Fleet, recently passed Cape St. Vincent with twenty-five well-found ships, among which are stated to be three of seven hundred tons, thirteen of three hundred, and the rest smaller. There he intercepted a ship trying to make its way to the Netherlands and carried it off together with its entire cargo. . . . Every one was utterly horrified at these tidings, than which nothing could be worse for the King and the Indian trade, seeing that with a favourable wind Drake must now be close to the Indian Islands (West Indies). At this juncture the ships from New Spain would certainly be loaded up and on their way, so that the Englishman would have them at his mercy. Don Melendez is neither sufficiently armed, nor has he enough equipment and men to face Drake. But the latter knows how much armament he requires and has made all necessary preparations. And the most annoying part of this affair is that this Hawkins could not have fitted out so numerous and so well equipped a fleet without the aid and secret consent of the Queen. This conflicts with the agreement for the sake of which the King sent an Envoy Extraordinary to the Queen of England. It is the nature and habit of this nation not to keep faith, so the Queen pretends that all has been done without her knowledge and desire. The French write that their King Francis, owing to the tricks played on him during his reign by the English, always had on his lips the following epigram:

> 'Anglicus, Anglicus est cui nunquam credere fas est,
> Tum tibi dicit ave, tanquam ab hoste cave.'

From V. Von Klarwill, *The Fugger News-letters 1568–1605*, 2nd series, trans. L. S. R. Byrne, John Lane, The Bodley Head, 1926, pp. 7–8

document 3

The making of English foreign policy

(a) *Sir Thomas Smith's* De Republica Anglorum, *written in 1565, provides a contemporary statement on the structure of government in the sixteenth century. Here is his description of the royal prerogative in foreign policy.*

The Prince whom I nowe call (as I have often before) the Monarch of Englande, King or Queene, hath absolutelie in his power the authoritie of warre and peace, to defie what Prince it shall please him, and to bid him warre, and againe to reconcile himselfe and enter into league or truce with him at his pleasure or the advice onely of his privie counsell. His privie counsell be chosen also at the Princes pleasure out of the nobilitie or baronie, and of the Knightes, and Esquiers, such and so many as he shal thinke good, who doth consult daily, or when neede is of the weightie matters of the Realme, to give therein to their Prince the best advice they can. The Prince doth participate to them all, or so many of them, as he shall thinke good, such legations and messages as come from forren Princes, such letters or occurrentes as be sent to himselfe or to his secretaries, and keepeth so many ambassades and letters sent unto him secret as he will, although these have a particular oth of a counceller touching faith and secrets administred unto them when they be first admitted into that companie.

From Thomas Smith, *De Republica Anglorum*, ed. Mary Dewar, Cambridge, 1982, p. 85

(b) *This letter from Sir William Cecil to Queen Elizabeth was written in 1559 or 1560 when the Council was divided over the question of whether to give open aid to the protestant lords in Scotland. Cecil, unlike Elizabeth and some other councillors, favoured a forward policy. His letter reveals the limitations of the royal minister in making policy.*

It may please your most Excellent Majesty, – With a sorrowfull harte and watery eies, I your poore servant and most lowlye subject, an unworthy Secretory, besech your Majesty to pardon this my lowlye suite, that considering the proceding in this matter for removing of the French out of Scotland doth not content your Majesty, and that I cannot with my conscience gyve any contrary advise, I may, with your Majestie's favor and clemency, be spared to entermeddle therein. And this I am forced to doo of necessitie, for I will never be a minister in any your Majestie's service, whereunto your owne mynd shall not be agreable, for thereunto I am sworne, to be a minister of your Majesty's determynations and not of myne owne, or of others, though they be never so many. And on the other part to serve your Majesty in any thyng that myself cannot allow, must nedes be an unprofitable service, and so untoward, as therin I wold be loth your Majesty should be deceyved.

And as for any other service, though it were in your Majesty's kytchen or garden, from the bottom of my harte I am ready without respect of estymation, welthe, or ease, to doo your Majesty's commandement to my lyve's end. Whereof I wish with all my poor sorrowfull hart, that your Majesty would make some proofe, for this I doo affyrme, that I have not had sence your Majesty's reigne, any one daye's joye, but in your Majesty's honor and weale.

From T. Wright, *Queen Elizabeth and Her Times*, London, 1838, vol. 1, pp. 24–25

document 4
Henry VII's treaty with Spain, 1489

The Treaty of Medina del Campo was signed by Ferdinand and Isabella on 28 March 1489. But Henry did not finally ratify it until 23 September 1490 when various additional articles were included.

1. A true friendship and alliance shall be observed henceforth between Ferdinand and Isabella, their heirs and subjects, on the one part, and Henry, his heirs and subjects, on the other part. They promise to assist one another in defending their present and future dominions against any enemy whatsoever. . . .
2. Neither party shall in any way favour the rebels of the other party, nor permit them to be favoured or stay in his dominions.
3. Mutual assistance to be given against all aggressors within three months after the assistance has been requested. The assisted party to pay the expenses, which are to be fixed by four knights, two from each side.
4. Henry is not permitted to assist Charles, King of France, or any other prince at war with Spain. Ferdinand and Isabella promise the same to Henry.
5. Henry is not to conclude peace, alliance or treaties with France, without the sanction of Ferdinand and Isabella, who, on their side, bind themselves to the same effect with respect to Henry.
6. As often as and whenever Ferdinand and Isabella make war with France, Henry shall do the same, and conversely. . . .
17. In order to strengthen this alliance the Princess Katharine is to marry Prince Arthur. The marriage is to be contracted *per verba de futuro* as soon as Katherine and Arthur attain the necessary age.

From A. F. Pollard, *The Reign of Henry VII from Contemporary Sources*, London, 1913, vol. 1, pp. 2–5

Henry VII and Brittany

This dispatch from the Collector de Giglis to Pope Innocent VIII on 28 January 1489 describes Henry's policy towards Brittany.

... his Majesty himself made many loving speeches about your Holiness, saying he had nothing more at heart, than when the preparations of Christendom shall be matured, to proceed against the Infidels; he added that he was not meditating anything against the King of the French, but he is compelled at present to defend the Breton interests, both on account of the immense benefits conferred on him by the late Duke in the time of his misfortunes, and likewise for the defence of his own kingdom; the affairs of Britanny being so bound up with those of England, that the latter are necessarily endangered by the Breton catastrophe; and that he has sent ambassadors to the King of the French for peace, which if effected, all will be well; but if not, he has determined to defend Britanny and the orphan Duchess with all his might.

Ambassadors have also been sent to the King of Castile, to confirm the confederacy which was well nigh concluded here, in which there is a clause about a marriage to be contracted between the only son of the King and one of the daughters of the aforesaid King of Castile.

An embassy has been dispatched to the King of the Romans and the Flemings to arrange matters at issue, or, if that may not be, at least to make friendship with both, or with one or other of them, whichever will consent to fair terms, so that trade, so long suspended between the parties, may be brought back into its accustomed channel.

The parliament, which has been summoned, will commence on the 13th of this month. Its chief care will be to make provision for the war, above all the necessary funds for its prosecution – a matter of no small difficulty, as for their acquirement, not only on the laity will a heavy burden be laid, but also on the clergy, who it is said, will be subjected to a tax of three-tenths.

From *Calendar of State Papers Venetian I 1202–1509*, pp. 177–8

document 6

A foreign observer's view of Henry VII

. . . this kingdom is perfectly stable, by reason, first, of the King's wisdom, whereof every one stands in awe; and, secondly, on account of the King's wealth, for I am informed that he has upwards of six millions of gold, and it is said that he puts by annually five hundred thousand ducats, which is of easy accomplishment, for his revenue is great and real, not a written schedule, nor does he spend anything. He garrisons two or three fortresses, contrary to the custom of his predecessors, who garrisoned no place. He has neither ordnance nor munitions of war, and his body guard is supposed not to amount to one hundred men. . . . He well knows how to temporise, as demonstrated by him before my arrival in this kingdom, when the French ambassadors wanted to go to Scotland under pretence of mediating for the peace, but he entertained them magnificently, made them presents, and sent them home without seeing Scotland; and now he sends one of his own gentlemen in waiting to France. The Pope is entitled to much praise, for he loves the King cordially, and strengthens his power by ecclesiastical censures, so that at all times rebels are excommunicated.

From *Calendar of State Papers Venetian I 1202–1509*, p. 261

document 7

Wolsey's aims in foreign policy

In 1518 Wolsey clearly desired peace, but his motives for seeking it are less clear.

(a) LETTER SIGNED 10 MARCH 1518
That it was expedient there should be peace between the Christian powers to which England was much inclined, and especially Cardinal Wolsey, who, when there was a question of hostilities, opposed them strenuously.

From *Calendar of State Papers Venetian II 1509–19*, p. 435

(b) LETTER SIGNED 24 SEPTEMBER 1518
The Cardinal stated that peace and confederacy would be concluded between the Kings of England and France, the Pope, the

Emperor, and the Catholic King. If any one of the allies took up arms or plotted against another of them, all the confederates were bound to defend the latter, at the cost of the petitioner for aid. Knowing the Cardinal to be greedy of glory and covetous of praise, [I] told him that he would obtain immortal fame by this alliance, for whereas the Pope had laboured to effect a quinquennial truce, his Lordship had made perpetual peace, and whereas such a union of the Christian powers was usually concluded at Rome this confederacy had been concluded in England, although the Pope was its head.

From *Calendar of State Papers Venetian II 1509–19*, p. 458

document 8
Wolsey and the Pope

This letter written by the Imperial ambassador in Rome in July 1520 demonstrates the Pope's desire for an English alliance and his strong antipathy to Wolsey.

The Pope is so desirous to conclude the alliance that if he is asked to make the Cardinal his legate in England, and if pressure be brought to bear upon him, he will nominate the Cardinal. Although there is no man on the face of the earth whom his Holiness detests so heartily as the Cardinal, he will be constituted legate if the Pope be given to understand that in no other way can he get out of the difficulties in which he is placed.

From *Calendar of State Papers Spanish 1509–25*, p. 309

document 9
Henry VIII's ambitions in France

On 26 March 1527, after Francis I's capture and defeat at the battle of Pavia, Henry told his ambassadors in France to congratulate the Emperor and suggest to him the invasion and partition of France.

And in this matter the said ambassadors may say that, the Emperor being contented to make the said personal invasion on that side, such ways may be taken, leving fortresses and strongholds, that the Emperor may come with his army unto Paris, where the King's Highness will not fail, God willing, to meet him; . . . At which

Paris, after the said personal meeting, the King's Grace may in this case take the crown of France; and the same had, His Grace, to show mutual correspondence of kindness unto the Emperor, shall give unto him all effectual assistance for attaining of his crown Imperial: wherein the said ambassadors shall use these degrees:

First, they shall say the King's Highness can in this case be contented to give the Emperor 5,000 archers at the King's charges, for five, or, rather than fail, for six months, or in the lieu and stead thereof, the sum of 100,000 crowns.

The second degree is, that the said ambassadors shall grant thereunto the sum of 150,000 crowns.

Thirdly, 200,000 crowns: and finally, if by none of these offers the Emperor can be induced to invade in person, meeting the King at Paris as afore, they shall say, as of themselves, that they doubt not but, the crown of France once had, the King's Highness will be contented in his own person to accompany the Emperor unto Rome. And if such general words will not satisfy the Emperor and his Council, the said ambassadors shall not let, all the residue of the King's desire in this point concurring with the same, to conclude the King's personal accompanying of the Emperor unto Rome, there to see the crown Imperial set on his head, giving his best assistance as well thereunto, as to the recovery of all such droits and rights as appertain to the Empire, whereof Italy is the chamber: of which glorious voyage the said ambassadors shall say is like to ensue unto the Emperor the whole monarchy of Christendom; for of his own inheritance he hath the realm of Spain, and a great part of Germany, the realms of Sicily and Naples, with Flanders, Holland, Zeeland, Brabant, and Hainault, and other his Low Countries; by election he hath the Empire, whereunto appertaineth almost all the rest of Italy, and many towns imperial in Germany and elsewhere; by the possibility apparent to come by my Lady Princess he should hereafter have England and Ireland, with the title to the superiority of Scotland, and in this case all France with the dependencies: so as the said Emperor, performing this voyage, and taking this way, should in process be peaceable lord and owner in manner of all Christendom; which the King's Grace can be contented the Emperor shall have, he concurring effectually with the King for recovery of his crown of France. . . .

As to the second, who should succeed in the realm of France, the French King and his line removed? The King's Highness verily trusteth that, his just title and right thereunto remembered and considered, the Emperor, since the treaties and alliances passed between the King's Grace and him, was never, ne is, of other mind but firmly to join with His Highness for recovery of the said crown; wherein the said ambassadors may, apart unto himself, put him in remembrance of his secret promise made, as well unto the King's Highness as to my Lord Legate, at sundry places and times: wherefore in this matter there is no question or ambiguity which may insurge, but that the French King taken or not taken, his army vanquished or not vanquished, one of the chief and principal things intended and convented by their confederation hath always been to expel the French King from his usurped occupation of the crown of France, and to conduce the King's Highness, as right requireth, unto the same. . . .

From M. St Clare Byrne (ed.), *The Letters of Henry VIII*, Cassell 1936, pp. 36–37

document 10

Henry and Scotland, 1543–44

(a) *Henry's ambassador to Scotland, Sir Ralph Sadler, advised Henry on how to handle the Scottish lords after the English victory at Solway Moss. Henry did not heed the advice. The letter is dated 20 March 1543.*

'Well,' quoth I, 'Mr Douglas,[1] the king's majesty hath had large offers, as ye know, both for the government of the realm, and to have the child[2] brought into his hands, with also the strong holds, according to your promises; and if your ambassadors should now come with mean things, not agreeable to his highness, you are a wise man, ye know what may ensue thereof.' 'Why,' quoth he, 'his majesty shall have the marriage offered to be contracted, and they have authority to conclude it; and having that first, the rest of his desires may follow in time. But for my part,' quoth he, 'I made no such promise as ye speak of; and they that made such promises, are not able to perform them. For surely,' quoth he, 'the noblemen will not agree to have her out of the realm, because she is their mistress; but they are content, that the king's majesty shall appoint some gentlemen of England, and some English ladies, to be here about her person, for her better tuition, at his majesty's pleasure; and this entry at the first may bring her wholly into his hands in short time; but I tell you,' quoth he, 'all things cannot be done at once. . . . And again,' quoth he, 'of the other party; if there be any motion now to take the governour[3] from his state, and to bring the government of this realm to the king of England, I assure you, it is impossible to be done at this time. For,' quoth he, 'there is not so little a boy but he will hurl stones against it, and the wives will handle their distaffs, and the commons universally will rather die in it, yea, and many noblemen and all the clergy be fully against it, ...'

1. Sir George Douglas. A Scot who had been exiled in England but was sent back by Henry VIII to his native country after Solway Moss to strengthen the English party in Scotland.
2. Mary Stuart.
3. James Hamilton, Earl of Arran.

From A. Clifford (ed.), *The State Papers of Sir Ralph Sadler*, Edinburgh, 1809, vol. 1, pp. 69–70

(b) *Henry made clear to the Earl of Hertford the punitive nature of his expedition into Scotland.*

It may further like your Lordship tunderstande, that the King's Majestie hath also seen your Devise for the Proclamation, which his Majestie surely thinketh to procede of a good Hart and Will to serve him; and we all think the same. And yet, forasmuch as if ye shulde cause the same to be proclaymed now at your furst entre, before youe wer sure how to fynde those of that Cuntrey, which ought to serve his Majestie, youe cannot then afterward burne and spoyle the Cuntrey with his Majesties Honour, having ones proclaymed his Majestie to be as it wer chief Governour of the Quene and Protector of the Realme; we think it better ye differre the same untill such Tyme, as you shall see that youe have the upperhande of the Ennemys, and the Mastery of the Cuntry in your Hande; and that youe have Experience that suche as shuld be the King's Majesties Freends there do joyne ernestly with youe; which failling youe may fall to burning, having proclaimed nothing openly before, that ought to let youe therefro in Honour. And this is our Advise, which your Lordship may ensue, or otherwise do, as Things shall ministre unto you occasion. Wherof youe, seeing them there at your Eye, shalbe able moche better to judge and use the Commoditye of the same presently, thenne we can here. We returne unto youe the Proclamation agayn, which his Majestie hath altred in one or twoo Things as youe shall perceyve by the same.

From S. Haynes, *A Collection of State Papers Relating to Affairs in the Reigns of King Henry VIII, King Edward VI, Queen Mary and Queen Elizabeth*, London, 1740, p. 21

document 11
William Paget's advice to Somerset and the Council on foreign policy, 28 April 1549

Albeit I knowe that with out myne advise your grace and the rest of my lordes can determyne the matter proponed by youe the last daye furst apart to me and then in counsaill concerninge your procedinges for Scotland: yet for discharge both of my dewtie of conscience and also bond of service to my soveraigne and countrey, I haue thought good with humble submission of my judgement to the wisedome of your grace and the rest of my lordes and others of the kinges majesties counsaill to saye myne opinion as foloweth. And furst I thincke that the suertie and honour of the kinges maistie and the realme is to be preferred above all other things; which surtiee and honour is not to be measured by any one present acte, as to take this or that place, oneles there be also a foresight of a certayne habilitie and power to kepe it stille and to defend throughly all other inconveniences which may grow by occasion of the same, for elles to seke honour by getting of a place, and afterward for lacke to be enforced to lose or leave the same againe, or ells to lose in the meane time some other thinge that shall countervaile two suche as yow thincke to get ys rather a reproche and a dishonour in the world, by whose judgement in meane thinges honour dishonour better and worse is determyned. When Boulogne was wonne the victory semed honourable at the furste and so dyd our entrey into warre after the death of the kinge upon Scotlande. But now having felt the charges of bothe to have bene so great and the inconvenience of them suche as we are not (for any thinge that I knowe) able to avoyde, the moste part of men forthincke the takinge of Boulogne and diverse wise men wishe that we had lived in the surceance of warre with Scotlande. When Boulogne was wonne yt was saide we shuld never haue good peace with Fraunce tille yt were restored. And when we beganne warre firste with Scotlande the French kinge said he wolde rather lose his realme then leave them. . . . Wherfore without peace with Scotlande I beleve that the French kinge will neuer be at peace with Englande. Then yf warre with Scotlande bringe warre with Fraunce, yt is good to consider whether we be hable to maintayne warre with Fraunce so many yeres as we shall make them wery to take parte with Scotlande. And yf we be, then maye we be the bolder to contynewe our conquest and fortifications in Scotlande. But if we be not I thincke we are not then to take more and fortefie more and in thende to be enforced to leave it over to your enemie, albeit the first parte *viz.* takinge, hath a visage of honor: yet the other parte *viz.* after waste of much tyme, spence of much money, losse of your people, to leave to your enemie, that which youe haue gotten, and to the kinge, his owne realme in mysery and beggerye when he shall enter him selfe to governement, ys a certayne and inevitable dishonour in the judgement of the worlde. . . . Youe do consider I am suer, how great a prince the French kinge ys. . . . And on the other side how we are exhausted and worne to the bones with these eight yeres warres both of men money and all other thinges for the warres your grace and my lordes knowe better then I, what credyt youe haue to borowe abrode, . . . and howe like we are to haue any helpe of your subjectes yow se presently before your eyes. As for the abandoninge of Hadington ys no dishonour but rather a wisedome and so reputed throughe the worlde . . . The king that deade is being a prince with longe continuance of great fame & reputacion, upon consideracion of his estate and condition at home could fynde in his herte to forbeare the warres with Scotlande, havinge the same querell that we pretende nowe, and yet was yt no dishonour to him at all. All I suppose (under correction) that if we who haue renewed the warres and wonne by them forbeare now further invasion for a tyme and stand to the defence of so muche of that which we haue wonne of Scotlande as our power will serve to, in respecte of our scarcitie, nother the Scottes nor any other prynce hath cause to thincke dishonour in us, and thoughe they dyd, for want of knowledge of our estate, yet must we do that we maye and are able to do, which me thincketh is very litle.

From B. L. Beer and S. M. Jack (eds.), *The Letters of William, Lord Paget of Beaudesert 1547–1563*, Camden Miscellany (vol. 25), 4th series, vol. 13, 1974, pp. 76–78

Mary's marriage to Philip II
document 12

The Spanish ambassador in England frequently warned Philip II of French plots to foil the projected marriage alliance.

It is important that your Highness make speed to come to this kingdom, not merely for the marriage, but for other private and public business. Unless your Highness comes before Lent, I doubt it may be difficult to induce the Queen to marry at that time, though his Majesty has taken steps to obtain the necessary dispensation from the Pope. It is feared that the English people may give trouble in the course of next summer on account of religion and also because they are irritated against the nobility and the Spanish match, but the councillors and principal vassals and nobles approve, provided your Highness comes before spring time and caresses the English with your wonted kindliness. You may be certain that the ill will of the heretics has been exploited by the French, who are fitting out a number of men-of-war on the Breton and Norman coasts with a view to trying to stop your Highness, so you must be accompanied by enough ships to defeat any surprise attack.

From *Calendar of State Papers Spanish 1554–58*, pp. 18–19

document 13
The Earl of Shrewsbury informs the Privy Council of the failure of the Scots to invade England, October 1557

It may please your honourable Lordships to be advertised; being in continual expectation, and laying daily wait of the Scots' entry into England; having our force prepared to defend them and annoy them, in such sort as has been signified to your Lordships, and I in readiness, with 1000 men, to have set forwards, and done as the occasion of the enemies' proceeding should have required; the Scots, whose enterprise had been much slacked with foul weather, after many consultations, and full determinations to enter England (being continually pricked forwards thereunto by the Queen and the French) were come the 17th of this instant to Eckford church, upon their driest frontiers towards Wark ... and hereupon encamping that night upon Hawdon Ridge, set forwards the next morning, being the 18th, and came near to Wark, having brought their ordnance over the Tweed; and skirmished before Wark, shewing such a likelihood to have given the approach that the Englishmen within, looking for the siege, had ramparted up the gates; yet that afternoon they brake up their camp, and retired back again and dispersed; and so their enterprise, begun with great bravery, is ended with dishonour and shame, praise be given to God therefore.

From E. Lodge, *Illustrations in British History*, London, 1838, vol. 1, p. 356

The loss of Calais

document 14

Lord Grey of Wilton, Governor of Guisnes, warned Mary of the danger to Calais from the French on 4 January 1558 and informed her of his need for reinforcements.

My most bounden duty humbly premised to your Majesty. Whereas I have heretofore always in effect written nothing to your Highness but good, touching the service and state of your places here; I am now constrained, with woful heart, to signify unto your Majesty these ensuing.

The French have won Newhaven Bridge, and thereby entered into all the Low Country and the marshes between this [Guisnes] and Calais. They have also won Rysbanke, whereby they be now master of that haven.

And this last night past, they have placed their ordnance of battery against Calais, and are encamped at St. Peter's Heath before it: so that I now am clean cut off from all relief and aid which I looked to have (both out of England, and from Calais) and know not how to have help by any means, either of men or victuals.

There resteth now none other way for the succour of Calais and the rest of your Highness's pieces on this side, but a power of men out of England, or from the King's Majesty [PHILIP II]; or from both, without delay, able to distress and keep them from victuals coming to them, as well by sea as land; which shall force them to leave their siege to the battle, or else drive them to a greater danger.

For lack of men out of England, I shall be forced to abandon the Town [of Guisnes], and take in the soldiers thereof for the Castle. I have made as good provision of victuals as I could, by any means, out of the country; with which, GOD willing! I doubt not to defend and keep this piece as long as any man, whosoever he be, having no better provision, and furniture of men and victuals than I have.

From Edward Arber, *Tudor Tracts, An English Garner*, ed. A. F. Pollard, Cooper Square, New York, 1964, p. 319

English aid to the Huguenots, 1562

document 15

(a) *This memorandum, dated 20 July 1562, was drafted by Sir William Cecil to draw attention to the dangers to England of a Guise victory in France.*

THE PERILLS GROWING UPPON THE OVERTHROW OF THE PRYNCE
OF CONDEE'S CAUSE.

The whole regyment of the crowne of Fraunce shall be in the hands
of the Guisians; and, to maynteane there faction, they will pleasure
the Kyng of Spayne in all that they maye. Hereuppon shall follow
a complott betwixt them twoo, to avance there owne pryvat causees;
the King of Spayne, to unhable the Howss of Navarr for ever from
clayming the kyngdom of Navarr; the Howss of Guife, to promote
there nece the Quene of Scotts to the crown of England. And for
doing therof twoo thyngs principally will be attempted: the mariadg
betwixt the Prynce of Spayne and the sayd Quene; and, in this
compact, the realme of Irland to be gyven in a praye to the King
of Spayne.

Whylest this is in work, and that the protestants rest as beholders
onely; the general counsell shall condemne all the protestants, and
gyve the kyngdoms and dominions therof to any other prynce that
shall invade them. In this meane tyme, all the papistes in England
shal be sollicited not to styrr; but to confirme there faction with
comefort, to gather monny, and to be redy to styrr at one instant,
when some forrayn force shall be redy to assayle this realme, or
Irland.

Whan the matter is brought to these termes, that the papists shall
have the upper hand; than will it be to late to seke to withstand it:
for than the matter shall be lyke a great rock of stone that is fallyng
downe from the topp of a mountayn, which whan it is comming
no force can stey.

Whosoever thynketh, that relentyng in relligion will aswage the
Guisians aspirations, they ar farr deceyved: for two appetites will
never be satisfyed, but with the thyng desyred; the desyre to have
such a kyngdom, as England and Scotland may make unyted; and
the cruell appetite of a Pope and his adherents to have his authorité
restablished fully, without any new daunger of attempt.

From Patrick Forbes, *A Full View of the Public Transactions in the Reign
of Queen Elizabeth*, London, 1741, vol. 2, p. 2

(b) *Elizabeth explained to Philip II on 22 September 1562 some of her
anxieties about the political and religious divisions in France.*

Suerly we have bene much trobled and perplexed from the beginning of these divisions in France, and upon diverse cawses: fyrst,
becawse we had a great compassion to see the yong King owr

brother so abused by his subjects, as his aucthoritie could not direct them to accord. Next thereto we feared, that herof might followe an universall troble to the rest of christiendome; considering, the quarrell was discovered and published to be for the matter of relligion. Lastly, which towcheth us most nearely and properly, we perceaved, that the Duke of Guise and his Howse was the principall head of one parte; and that they daylie so increased their force, as in the end they became commaunders of all things in France; and theruppon such manner of hostile dealyng used, in diverse sorts, against our subjects and merchants in sondry parts of France, as we were constreyned to looke abowte us, what perill might ensue to our owne estate and contrey.

And thereupon could we not forgett, how they were the very parties that evicted Callice [Calais] from this crowne; a matter of continuall greef to this realme, and of glory to them; and unjustly observyd also the first capitulations, for the reddition thereof into there hand. Nether cold we forgett, how hardly by their meanes we were delt withall at the conclusion of the peace at Casteau in Cambresy [Câteau-Cambrésis].

From *ibid.*, vol. 2, p. 53

The Spanish treasure ships

document 16

Having asked the Queen and Cecil for the return of the treasure ships to their owners, de Spes reported to Alva their response in a letter dated 22 December 1568 and urged immediate reprisals.

Cecil was very grave about it, as also was the earl of Leicester. Sometimes they said they were guarding it for his Majesty, and sometimes that it belonged to other persons; but they would not say whether they had sent similar orders to Plymouth and Falmouth. Their refusal to declare themselves on the point, however, proves that they have done so. They consulted the Queen and then said that the money was in safe keeping and no other answer could then be given. I pressed for an audience and they told me to ask again after dinner, they in the meanwhile being closeted with the ambassador of the prince of Condé, so that I could get no reply from them. The Chamberlain was requested to go and ask the Queen, which he went in to do at once, and came out very much irritated, saying he had not ventured to ask her Majesty for audience as she was not in the habit of granting it on such days. The affair is thus in a very bad way and these people are determined to do any wickedness, so this money will not be recovered. I pray your Excellency do not fail to seize all English property and send word to Spain instantly for them to do the same there.

From *Calendar of State Papers Spanish 1568–79*, p. 91

document 17

Scotland, 1570

Sussex's first raid into Scotland was ostensibly to punish the Scottish Marian lords harbouring the English rebels who had fled after their abortive rising in 1569. Sussex here was urging Cecil to persuade the Queen to make a decision on further action. He wanted to give aid to the protestant lords against the Marians but Elizabeth found difficulty in determining future policy.

The time passeth away, and therefore it were good her Majesty would resolve what she will do; for as if she will restore the S. Q. it were no good policy to have me shew countenance on the other side, so, if she will maintain the other side, and command me to join with them, I will, with allowance of 300 carriage horses, make all men within 30 miles of the borders to obey that authority, or I will not leave a stone house for any of them to sleep in in surety that shall refuse; and, if her Majesty command me to pass further, I will, with the help of Morton,[1] deliver the castle of Edinburgh, or any other in Scotland, to the hands of any in Scotland whom Morton, with her Majesty's consent, shall appoint to receive them. These matters have too long slept; it is time now to wake; and, therefore, good Mr Secretary, sound the Queen's mind fully; and if she intend to restore the Scotch Queen, advise her to do it in convenient sort, and suffer me not to put my finger in the fire without cause, and her to be drawn into it by such degrees as are neither honourable nor sure; and if she will set up the other side, and make open shew thereof, let her command what she will, and it shall be done, or I will lie by it.

1. Morton: James Douglas 4th Earl of Morton, one of the Lords of the congregation, became Regent at the end of 1572.

From E. Lodge, *Illustrations of British History in the Reign of Elizabeth*, London, 1838, vol. 1, p. 506

document 18

The Netherlands, 1572

In this 'Memorial for Matters of Flanders' drawn up in June 1572, Burghley expressed his concern that the French should not obtain a foothold in the Netherlands.

If upon these and other intelligences it appear manifest that the Duke of Alva is sufficiently prepared and able to resist all attempts, so as he may detain his master's countries from the conquest of the French, then it is like to be best for England to let both sides alone for a time; otherwise the French may be offended and the Spaniard not made sure, and if they accord we shall be sure of neither.

If it appear that the Duke is not able to defend his master's countries from the French and that the French begin to possess any part of them, and especially the maritime parts, then it is like that the French, increasing their dominance, may be too potent neighbours for us and therefore [it] may be good for us to use all the means that may conveniently be, to stay that course.

If the French proceed to seek to possess the maritime coasts and frontiers it seemeth to be good that by some good means the Duke of Alva were informed secretly of the Queen's Majesty's disposition to assist the king his master by all honourable means she might in the defence of his inheritance, so as it may appear to her that he will discharge his subjects of their intolerable oppression, restore them to their ancient liberties, reconcile his nobility to him, deliver them from the fear of the Inquisition and continue with her Majesty the ancient league for amity and traffic in as ample sort as any others, dukes of Burgundy, heretofore have done.

From Kervyn de Lettenhove, *Relations politiques des Pays-Bas et L'Angleterre*, Brussels, 1891, vol. 6, p. 421

document 19

The Netherlands, 1578

Walsingham, Elizabeth's ambassador to the Estates in the summer of 1578, wrote regularly to his fellow councillors of events in the Netherlands, in the hope that they might urge Elizabeth to intervene – but to no avail.

(a) WALSINGHAM'S LETTER TO SUSSEX DATED 23 JULY 1578
For what case things stand here and what will become of these

countries in case Her Majestie withdraws her promised assistance from them, we have so largely set down in our general letter to Your Lordship and the rest of My Lords as I think it needless to make any recital therof. Truly, my Lord, if Her Majesty do not presently resolve to take an other course then I perceive (to my great grief) she is inclined to, I see apparently that this country will become french.

From *ibid.*, vol. 10, p. 631

(b) LEICESTER'S LETTER TO WALSINGHAM DATED 1 AUGUST 1578

I am sorry to see both our travail fall out to no better effect. Good Mr Secretary, it grieveth me, I cannot say how much, that I am neither able to satisfy that expectation in you I would most gladly, nor yet take comfort my self in our proceedings here. It is no small alteration I find in Her Majesties disposition, since we were at Otland and Windsor, toward the state of those countries. How loth she is to come to any manner of dealings that way, specially to be at any charges, it is very strange.

From *ibid.*, vol. 10, p. 678

document 20

The Anjou marriage scheme, 1578

The Council was divided over the proposed marriage.
(a) *Sussex was its leading proponent, as he demonstrates in this letter to Elizabeth.*

Touching the marriage (if your Majesty in your own heart can like of it, which I leave to God and you) I find these commodities to follow. Your alliance with the house of France; whereby (besides all likelihood that the French King will not attempt any thing to the prejudice of you and his brother) you shall be assured, by yourself and your husband, to have such a party in France as the French King shall not be able, nor shall not dare, to attempt directly or indirectly any thing against you. You shall, by yourself, and your husband, be able to assure the Protestants of France from peril of massacre by the Papists, and the King from any perilous action by them; and so, by your means, keep the King and his people in unity and Christian peace. You shall take away, and suppress, all practise for competition,[1] for Popery, or any other seditious cause, at home or abroad; and so shall, at home and abroad, assure your person, and your state, from all perils that by man's judgement might grow any ways to you by France. You shall, also, by the help of your husband, be able to compel the King of Spain to take reasonable conditions of his subjects in the Low Countries, and the States to take reasonable conditions of their King, so as he may have that which before God and man doth justly belong to him, and they may enjoy their liberties, freedoms, and all other things that are fit for their quiet and surety . . . . And herewith, for the more surety of all persons and matters, yourself may have in your own hands some maritime port, to be by you kept, at the charge of the King of Spain; and your husband may have some frontier towns in like sort; and both to be continued for such a number of years as may bring a settling of surety to all respects; by which means you shall also be delivered from perils, at home and abroad, that may grow from the King of Spain. And if you like not of this course in dealing for the Low Countries, you may join with your husband, and so, between you, attempt to possess the whole Low Countries, and draw the same to the Crown of England if you have any child by him; or, if you have none, to divide them between the realms of England and France as shall be meetest for either; but, to be plain with your Majesty, I do not think this course to be so just, so godly, so honourable, nor, when it is looked into the bottom, so sure for you and your State as the other, although at the first sight it doth perhaps carry in shew some plausibility.

1. Competition for the succession to the Crown of England: alluding to the pretensions of the Queen of Scots.

From E. Lodge, *Illustrations of British History in the Reign of Elizabeth*, London, 1838, vol. 2, p. 109–11

(b) *Amongst the body of writings against the marriage was a famous letter written by Sir Philip Sidney, Leicester's nephew.*

As for this man, as long as he is but Monsieur in might and a Papist in profession, he neither can nor will greatly stead you. And if he grow king, his defence will be like Ajax' shield, which weighed down rather than defended those that bore it.

Against contempt at home, if there be any, which I will never believe, let your excellent virtues of piety, justice and liberality daily, if it be possible, more and more shine. Let some such particular actions be found out (which is easy, as I think, to be done) by which you may gratify all the hearts of your people. Let those in whom you find trust, and to whom you have committed trust in your weighty affairs, be held up in the eyes of your subjects. Lastly, doing as you do, you shall be as you be: the example of princes, the ornament of this age, the comfort of the afflicted, the delight of your people, the most excellent fruit of all your progenitors, and the perfect mirror to your posterity.

From K. Duncan-Jones and J. Van Dorsten (eds), *Miscellaneous Prose of Sir Philip Sidney*, Oxford University Press, 1973, pp. 56–57.

document 21
Leicester's instructions for his expedition to the Netherlands, December 1585

To have care that her majesties subjectes serving under his lordship maie be well governed, and to use all good meanes to redresse the confused government of those countreys, and that some better forme might be established amongst them.

Touchinge the good ruling of her majesties subjectes, his lordship is directed to bend his course, during his charg there, rather to make a defensive then an offensyve warr, and not in any sort to hazard a battaile without great advantage. . . .

To lett the states understand, that, where by their commissioneres they made offer unto her majestie, first, of the soueraintie of those countreyes, which for sundrie respects she did not accept, secondlie, unto her protection, offring to be absolutelie gouerned by such as her majestie wold appoint and send ouer to be her lieftenaunt. That her majestie, although she would not take soe much uppon her as to comaund them in such absolute sort, yet unlesse they should shew themselves forward to use the advise of her majestie to be delivered unto them by her lieftenaunte, to work amongst them a faire unitie and concurrence for their owne defence, in liberall taxacions and good husbanding of their contribucions, for the more speedie atteyninge of a peace, her majestie wold think her favours unworthelye bestowed upon them.

To offer all his lordships travaile, care, and endevour, to understand their estates, and to geve them advice, from tyme to tyme, in that which maie be for the suretie of their estate and her majésties honour.

From J. Bruce (ed.), *Correspondence of Robert Dudley, Earl of Leycester . . . 1585 and 1586*, Camden Society, 27(1844), pp. 12–15

document 22

English aid to Henry of Navarre

Henry of Navarre was here replying to Elizabeth's request for a place in Brittany to act as a supply base for the English troops assisting him against Spain.

Considering the humours of some of his Catholic councillors, he could not assent to yielding Brest or St. Malo in particular, but would conclude that the first port town to be taken from the enemy should be delivered to Her Majesty for the retreat of her people. He hoped the Queen would not now forsake him, knowing how far she was interested in the common cause. He knew well what would immediately result for England if the Spanish King became King of France. 'Her Majesty made war at this time good cheap against so great enemy . . . and [he] wished that he had such another fool as Her Majesty had of him to make wars against the King of Spain, that he might look out at the window, as she doth now, and behold the tragedies between him and his enemies now in action.' He also knew how much it would import her to have so evil a neighbour as the Spaniard in Brittany. He was unwilling to lose so fair a part of his kingdom and he would do all he could to defend it. . . . Henry wanted to know whether the Queen might be moved to send him 2,000 men more for one month, in case Parma should return to give him battle. Wilkes and Unton said that she was disposed rather to revoke those already in France. The King said that with such help he would undertake to overthrow Parma and take Rouen, whereby he might draw into his purse 300,000 *livres* yearly over and above his present revenue. By settling the traffic there he would be able to furnish himself at all times with money to supply his extremities.

From R. B. Wernham (ed.), *List and Analysis of State Papers, Foreign Series, Elizabeth I*, vol. 3, June 1591–April 1592, p. 380, paragraph 665, HMSO

Bibliography

The bibliography is of necessity selective, and includes in the main only works referred to in the text.

PRINTED PRIMARY SOURCES

1   Brewer, J. S., *et al.*, *Letters and Papers, Foreign and Domestic, of the Reign of Henry VIII*, 21 vols, 1862–1910; Addenda, 1929–32

2   Bruce, John, *Correspondence of Robert Dudley, Earl of Leycester . . . 1585 and 1586*, Camden Society, 27(1844)

3   *Calendar of State Papers, Foreign, Edward, Mary and Elizabeth*, ed. W. Turnbull and J. Stevenson, 1861–63

4   *Calendar of State Papers Relating to Scotland and Mary, Queen of Scots, 1547–1603*, ed. J. Bain, 1898–1969

5   *Calendar of State Papers Spanish*, ed. G. A. Bergenroth, P. de Gayángos and M A. S. Hume, 1862–99

6   *Calendar of State Papers Venetian*, ed. R. Brown and G. C. Bentinck, 1864–90

7   *Cabala, Sive Scrinia Sacra*, 1691

8   Clifford, A., ed., *The State Papers and Letters of Sir Ralph Sadler*, 2 vols, Edinburgh, 1809

9   *A Collection of Scarce and Valuable Tracts . . . of the Late Lord Somers*, 2nd edn, ed. Walter Scott, vol. 1, London, 1809

10 Digges, Dudley, *The Compleat Ambassador*, etc., London, 1655

11 Hay, D. ed., *Anglica Historia by Polydore Vergil*, Camden Society, 3rd series, 74(1950)

12 Haynes, Samuel, and Murdin, William, eds, *Collection of State Papers . . . Left by William Cecil, Lord Burghley*, 2 vols, London, 1740–59

13 Kervyn de Lettenhove, *Relations politiques des Pays-Bas et L'Angleterre . . .*, 11 vols, Brussels, 1888–1900

14 Lodge, E., *Illustrations of British History*, 3 vols, London, 1838

15 Pollard, A. F., *The Reign of Henry VII from Contemporary Sources*, 3 vols, Longman, 1913–14

SECONDARY SOURCES: BOOKS

16 Alexander, Michael van Cleave, *The First of the Tudors: A Study of Henry VII and his Reign*, Croom Helm, 1981

17 Andrews, K. R., *Elizabethan Privateering*, Cambridge University Press, 1964

18 Andrews, K. R., *Drake's Voyages*, Weidenfeld & Nicolson, 1967

19 Beer, Barrett L., *Northumberland: The Political Career of John Dudley*, Kent State University Press, 1974

20 Bush, M. L., *The Government Policy of Protector Somerset*, Edward Arnold, 1975

21 Chambers, D. S., *Cardinal Bainbridge in the Court of Rome 1509–1514*, Oxford University Press, Oxford Historical Series, 2nd series, 1965

22 Chrimes, S. B., *Henry VII*, Eyre Methuen, 1972

23 Connell-Smith, G., *Forerunners of Drake: A Study of English Trade with Spain in the Early Tudor Period*, Longman, 1954

24 Conway, A., *Henry VII's Relations with Scotland and Ireland 1485–1498*, Cambridge University Press, 1932

25 Corbett, J. S., *Drake and the Tudor Navy*, 2 vols, 2nd edn, Longman, 1899

26 Crowson, P. S., *Tudor Foreign Policy*, Adam & Charles Black, 1973

27 Cruickshank, C. G., *Army Royal. Henry VIII's Invasion of France 1513*, Clarendon Press, 1969

28 Cruickshank, C. G., *The English Occupation of Tournai 1513–19*, Clarendon Press, 1971

29 Cruickshank, C. G., *Elizabeth's Army*, Oxford University Press, 1966

30 Dietz, F. C., *English Government Finance, 1485–1558*, University of Illinois Press, 1921

31 Donaldson, G., *Scotland: James V to James VII*, Edinburgh History of Scotland, Oliver & Boyd, 1965

32 Donaldson, G., *Mary Queen of Scots*, English Universities Press, 1974

33 Elliott, J. H., *Europe Divided*, Fontana, 1968

34 Elton, G. R., *Reform and Reformation 1509–1558*, Edward Arnold, 1977

35 Elton, G. R., *Reformation Europe 1517–1559*, Fontana, 1963

36 Fletcher, Anthony R., *Tudor Rebellions*, Longman, Seminar Studies in History, 3rd edn 1983

37 Gammon, S. R., *Statesman and Schemer: William, First Lord Paget, Tudor Minister*, David & Charles, 1973

38 Harbison, E. Harris, *Rival Ambassadors at the Court of Queen Mary*, Princeton University Press, 1940

39 Harvey, Nancy Lenz, *Thomas, Cardinal Wolsey*, Macmillan, 1980

40 Hill, D. J., *A History of Diplomacy in the International Development of Europe*, New York, 1962

41 Hoskins, W. G., *The Age of Plunder: the England of Henry VIII, 1500–1547*, Longman, 1976

42 Jones, N. L., *Faith by Statute: Parliament and the Settlement of Religion 1559*, Royal Historical Society, 1982

43 Jones, W. R. D., *The Mid-Tudor Crisis, 1539–1563*, Macmillan, 1973

44 Jordan, W. K., *Edward VI: The Young King*, Allen & Unwin, 1968

45 Jordan, W. K., *Edward VI: The Threshold of Power*, Allen & Unwin, 1970

46 Knecht, R. J., *Francis I*, Cambridge University Press, 1982

47 Lander, J. R., *Government and Community: England 1450–1509*, Edward Arnold, 1980

48 Levine, Mortimer, *Tudor Dynastic Problems 1460–1571*, Allen & Unwin, 1973

49 Loades, D. M., *The Reign of Mary Tudor: Politics, Government, and Religion in England 1553–58*, Ernest Benn, 1979

50 Loades, D. M., *Two Tudor Conspiracies*, Cambridge University Press, 1965

51 Lockyer, R., *Henry VII*, Longman, Seminar Studies in History, 2nd edn 1983

52 Lloyd, H., *The Rouen Campaign 1590–92*, Clarendon Press, 1973

53 MacCaffrey, W. T., *The Shaping of the Elizabethan Regime*, Cape, 1969

54 MacCaffrey, W. T., *Queen Elizabeth and the Making of Policy 1572–88*, Princeton University Press, 1981

55 Maltby, William S., *The Black Legend in England: the Development of Anti-Spanish Sentiment, 1558–1660*, Duke University Press, 1971

56 Mattingly, G., *The Defeat of the Spanish Armada*, Cape, 1959

57 Mattingly, G., *Renaissance Diplomacy*, Cape, 1955

58 Millar, Gilbert John, *Tudor Mercenaries and Auxiliaries 1485–1547*, University Press of Virginia, 1980

59 Merriman, R. B., *Life and letters of Thomas Cromwell*, 2 vols, Clarendon Press, 1902

60 Neale, Sir John, *Elizabeth I and her Parliaments*, 2 vols, Cape, 1953

61 Parker, G., *The Army of Flanders and the Spanish Road 1567–1659*, Cambridge University Press, 1972

62 Parker, G., *The Dutch Revolt 1548–1648*, Allen Lane, 1977

63 Parker, G., *Ten Studies: Spain and the Netherlands 1559–1659*, Fontana, 1979

64 Parmiter, G. de C., *The King's Great Matter: a Study of Anglo-Papal Relations, 1527–1534*, Longman, 1967

65 Pollard, A. F., *Henry VIII*, Longman, 1951 edn

66 Pollard, A. F., *Wolsey*, Longman, 1929

67 Pollard, A. F., *England under Protector Somerset*, Ballantyne Press, 1900

68 Prescott, H. F. M., *Mary Tudor*, Eyre & Spottiswoode, 2nd edn 1952

69 Ramsay, G. D., *The City of London in International Politics at the Accession of Queen Elizabeth*, Manchester University Press, 1975

70 Ramsay, G. D., *English Overseas Trade During the Centuries of Emergence*, Macmillan, 1957

71 Ramsey, P., *Tudor Economic Problems*, Gollancz, 1963

72 Read, Conyers, *Mr Secretary Walsingham and the Policy of Queen Elizabeth*, 3 vols, Oxford University Press, 1925

73 Read, Conyers, *Mr Secretary Cecil and Queen Elizabeth*, Cape, 1965

74 Read, Conyers, *Lord Burghley and Queen Elizabeth*, Cape, 1965

75 Russell, Conrad, *The Crisis of Parliaments: English History 1509–1660*, Oxford University Press, 1971

76 Scarisbrick, J. J., *Henry VIII*, Eyre & Spottiswoode, 1968

77 Slavin, A. J., *Politics and Profit: a Study of Sir Ralph Sadler, 1507–1547*, Cambridge University Press, 1966

78 Smith, A. G. R., *The Government of Elizabethan England*, Edward Arnold, 1967

79 Sutherland, N. M., *The Huguenot Struggle for Recognition*, Yale University Press, 1980

80 Sutherland, N. M., *The Massacre of Saint Bartholomew and the European Conflict 1559–1572*, Macmillan, 1973

81 Storey, R. L., *The Reign of Henry VII*, Blandford Press, 1968

82 Tittler, R., *Nicholas Bacon*, Cape, 1976

83 Tittler, R., *The Reign of Mary I*, Longman, Seminar Studies in History, 1983

84 Tjernagel, N. S., *Henry VIII and the Lutherans*, Concordia, St Louis, 1965

85 Tytler, P. F., *England under the Reigns of Edward VI and Mary*, Richard Bentley, London, 1839

86 Wernham, R. B., *Before the Armada: the Growth of English Foreign Policy 1485–1588*, Cape, 1966

87 Wernham, R. B., *The Making of Elizabethan Foreign Policy*, University of California Press, 1980

88 Wilkie, W. E., *The Cardinal Protectors of England: Rome and the Tudors before the Reformation*, Cambridge University Press, 1974

89 Williams, N., *The Cardinal and the Secretary*, Weidenfeld & Nicolson, 1975

90 Williams, P., *The Tudor Regime*, Clarendon Press, 1979

91 Wilson, C., *Queen Elizabeth and the Revolt of the Netherlands*, Macmillan, 1970

SECONDARY SOURCES: ARTICLES AND ESSAYS

92 Beer, B. L., 'The Myth of the Wicked Duke and the Historical John Dudley', *Albion*, 11 (1979)

93 Black, J. B., 'Queen Elizabeth, the Sea Beggars and the Capture of Brille, 1572', *English Historical Review*, 46 (1931)

94 Chambers, D. S., 'Cardinal Wolsey and the Papal Tiara', *Bulletin of the Institute of Historical Research*, 38 (1965)

95 Cooper, J. P., 'Henry VII's Last Years Reconsidered', *Historical Journal*, 2 (1959)

96 Davies, C. S. L., 'England and the French War, 1557–9', in J. Loach and R. Tittler (eds), *The Mid-Tudor Polity c. 1540–1560*, Macmillan, 1980

97 Glasgow, Jr, Tom, 'The Navy in Philip and Mary's War 1557–1559', *Mariner's Mirror*, 53 (1967)

98 Glasgow, Jr, Tom, "The Maturing of Naval Administration, 1556–1564', *Mariner's Mirror*, 56 (1970)

99 Goring, J. J., 'Social Change and Military Decline in Mid-Tudor England', *History*, 60 (June 1975)

100 Gwyn, P., 'Wolsey's Foreign Policy: The Conferences at Calais and Bruges Reconsidered', *Historical Journal*, 23 (1980)

101 Head, David M., 'Henry VIII's Scottish Policy: A Reassessment', *The Scottish Historical Review*, 61 (April 1982)

102 Kouri, E. I., 'Elizabethan England and Europe: 40 Unprinted Letters from Elizabeth I to Protestant Powers', *Bulletin of the Institute of Historical Research*, Special Supplement no. 12 (Nov. 1982)

103 MacCaffrey, W. T., 'The Anjou Match and the Making of Elizabethan Foreign Policy', in Peter Clark *et al.* (eds), *The English Commonwealth 1547–1640*, Leicester University Press, 1979

104 Mackie, J. D., 'Henry VIII and Scotland', *Transactions of the Royal Historical Society*, 4th series, 29 (1947)

105 Mattingly, G., 'An Early Non-Aggression Pact', *Journal of Modern History*, 10 (1938)

106 Neale, J. E., 'Elizabeth and the Netherlands 1586–7', *English Historical Review*, 45 (1930)

107 Pollitt, R., 'John Hawkins' Troublesome Voyages. Merchants, Bureaucrats and the Origins of the Slave Trade', *Journal of British Studies*, 12 (May 1973)

108 Potter, D. L., 'The Treaty of Boulogne and European Diplomacy 1549–50', *Bulletin of the Institute of Historical Research*, 55 (1982)

109 Read, Conyers, 'Queen Elizabeth's Seizure of Alba's Pay Ships', *Journal of Modern History*, 5 (1933)

110 Read, Conyers, 'Walsingham and Burghley in Queen Elizabeth's Privy Council', *English Historical Review*, 28 (1913)

111 Russell, J. G., 'The Search for Universal Peace: the Conferences at Calais and Bruges 1521', *Bulletin of the Institute of Historical Research*, 44 (1971)

112 Scammell, G. V., 'Shipowning in the Economy and Politics of Early Modern England', *Historical Journal*, 15 (1972)

113 Weikel, A., 'The Marian Council Revisited', in J. Loach and R. Tittler (eds), *The Mid-Tudor Polity c. 1540–1560*, Macmillan, 1980

114 Wernham, R. B., 'Queen Elizabeth and the Portugal Expedition of 1589', *English Historical Review*, 66 (1951)

115 Wernham, R. B., 'Elizabethan War Aims and Strategy', in S. T. Bindoff, *et al*, (eds), *Elizabethan Government and Society*, Athlone Press, 1961

116 Wernham, R. B., 'English Policy and the Revolt of the Netherlands', in J. S. Bromley and E. H. Kossman (eds), *Britain and the Netherlands*, Chatto and Windus, 1960

UNPUBLISHED THESES
117 Bush, M., 'The Rise to Power of Edward Seymour, Protector Somerset 1500–1547', Cambridge University Ph.D., 1965

118 Campbell, Dana Scott, 'English Foreign Policy 1509–21', Cambridge University Ph.D., 1980

119 Doran, S. M., 'The Political Career of Thomas Radcliffe, 3rd Earl of Sussex (1526?–1583)', London University Ph.D., 1977

120 Goring, J. J., 'The Military Obligations of the English People, 1511–1558', London University Ph.D., 1955

121 Potter, D. L., 'Diplomacy in the Mid 16th Century. England and France 1536–1550', Cambridge University Ph.D., 1973

RECENT PUBLICATIONS

122 Wernham, R. B., *After the Armada: Elizabethan England and the Struggle for Western Europe 1588–95*, Clarendon Press, Oxford, 1984

123 Adams, S., 'The Queen Embattled' in S. Adams (ed.), *Queen Elizabeth I, Most Politick Princess*, History Today Production, 1984

124 Andrews, K., *Trade, Plunder and Settlement*, Cambridge University Press, 1984

125 Palliser, D. M., *The Age of Elizabeth. England under the Later Tudors, 1547–1603*, Longman, 1983

126 Quinn, D. B. and Ryan, A. N., *England's Sea Empire 1550–1642*, Allen and Unwin, 1983

127 Ramsay, G. D., 'The Foreign Policy of Elizabeth I' in Haigh, C. (ed.) *The Reign of Elizabeth I*, Macmillan, 1984

128 Sutherland, N., 'The Foreign Policy of Queen Elizabeth, the Sea Beggars and the Capture of Brill, 1572' in N. Sutherland, *Princes, Politics and Religion, 1547–1589*, Hambledon Press, 1984

Glossary

Cortes The representative institution of each of the Kingdoms of Spain and Portugal

Curia Court

Estates – General The national representative assembly

Fief Territory held in vassalage

General Council of the Church An assembly of the most important representatives of the church, held irregularly, to discuss reform. In the mid-fifteenth century the Council held at Basle usurped the authority of the Pope; henceforeward Popes treated the call for a General Council with great suspicion.

Hanse A league of North German and Baltic trading towns

Huguenots French Calvinists

Legatus a latere The highest kind of papal legate. He was armed with papal authority and his acts were like those of the Pope himself.

Letters of marque Authorisation granted by governments to sea captains which allowed them to attack enemy shipping. Those who held and used letters of marque were *privateers*; those without them who plundered ships were *pirates*.

Malcontents A group of Catholic rebels in the Southern Netherlands who looked to the Duke of Anjou to help them in their struggle against the Spanish government

Politiques A group of moderates in France during the civil wars who supported the monarchy and opposed extreme protestantism and Catholicism alike

Stadtholder The lieutenant governor of provinces in the Netherlands

Staple A town appointed by royal authority in which a group of merchants had exclusive rights of purchase over certain classes of goods to be exported

Index

Alençon, Francis, Duke of (later Duke of Anjou), 2, 12, 67, 68, 69, 75, 76–7, 82, 103, 104
Alva, Duke of, 61, 62, 64, 100, 102
'Amicable Grant', 12, 31
Anjou, Duke of, *see* Alençon and Henry III of France
Antwerp, 4–5, 46, 66, 74, 76, 84
Armada, the Spanish, 77, 78, 79
army, organisation of the, 7–9, 79

Berwick, Treaty of, 58
Blois, Treaty of, 63, 70, 73
Boleyn, Anne, 31, 34, 35
Boulogne, 8, 16, 34, 44, 45, 48, 49, 95
Brandon, Charles, Duke of Suffolk, 27, 30, 44
Brittany, 1, 10, 15–16, 18, 22, 64, 74, 89, 106
Burghley, Lord, *see* Cecil, William
Burgundy, 1, 4, 13, 18, 24, 102; Margaret of Burgundy, 17, 18, 19; Philip of Burgundy, 17, 18, 19–20, 21; *see also* Netherlands
Bush, M, 40

Calais, 1, 4, 8, 16, 26, 34, 39, 44, 47, 50, 51, 53, 54–5, 56, 58, 59, 70, 82, 98, 100; conference at Calais 1521, 29–30
Campeggio, Cardinal, 28
Câteau-Cambrésis, Treaty of, 2, 55–6, 58, 100
Catherine of Aragon, 15, 17, 20, 21, 24, 32, 35, 88
Catherine de Medici, 58, 70, 71
Cecil, William, Lord Burghley, 14, 57, 58, 62, 73, 74, 75, 84, 87, 98, 100, 101, 102
Charles V, Holy Roman Emperor and King of Spain, 1–2, 4, 21, 26, 27, 28,

29, 30, 31, 32, 33, 34, 35, 36, 37, 39, 41, 45, 47, 48, 51, 60, 66, 81, 91
Charles VIII of France, 1, 16, 18, 88, 89
Charles IX of France, 71, 72, 74
Cleves, 36–7, 83
Coligny, Gaspard de, 2, 74
Courtenay, Edward, Earl of Devon, 50–1
Cromwell, Thomas, 13, 14, 36, 37
Crowson, P. S., 81, 82

debasement of the currency, 11, 46
Denmark, 5, 35, 36
Don John of Austria, 66, 67
Drake, Francis, 6, 10, 14, 68, 69, 70, 76, 77, 79, 85, 86
Dudley, John, Lord Lisle, Earl of Warwick, Duke of Northumberland, 5, 9, 13, 38, 45, 49–50, 54
Dudley, Robert, Earl of Leicester, 9, 12, 58, 61, 64, 67, 70, 73, 74, 76, 77, 100, 103, 104, 105–6

Edinburgh, Treaty of, 56
Edward VI of England, 43, 46
Elizabeth I of England, 5, 6, 8, 9, 10, 12, 13, 14, 55–80, 81, 82, 83, 87, 99–100, 101, 102, 103–4, 105, 106
Étaples, Treaty of, 16, 18, 23

Farnese, Alexander, Prince of Parma, 2, 68, 69, 77
Ferdinand of Aragon, 1, 16, 20, 21, 22, 23, 24, 27, 88, 89
Flanders, *see* Netherlands and Burgundy
Flodden, battle of, 24
Francis I of France, 27, 28, 29, 31, 32, 33, 34, 35, 36, 37, 41, 44, 45, 47, 86, 90, 91, 92
Francis II of France, 48, 57, 58

Gardiner, Stephen, Bishop of
Winchester, 37, 51, 53
Greenwich, Treaties of, 43
Guinea, 5, 85
Guise, family of, 57, 58, 60, 69, 70, 71,
73, 78, 98–100; Duke of, 53, 54, 55;
Mary of, 40, 57

Hampton Court, Treaty of, 59
Hawkins, John, 6, 9, 10, 61, 62, 78,
85–6
Henry II of France, 47, 48, 49, 51, 53,
54, 56, 57, 95
Henry III of France, until 1574 duke of
Anjou, 63, 68, 69, 70, 75–6, 103
Henry IV of France, Henry of Navarre,
2, 69, 71, 78, 82, 106
Henry VII of England, 4, 5, 6, 9, 12, 13,
15–22, 82, 88, 89, 90
Henry VIII of England, 7, 9, 12, 14, 16,
20, 21, 23–46, 81, 82, 83, 90, 91, 92,
93, 94, 96
Hertford, *see* Seymour, Edward
Holy Leagues, 16, 18, 23; of Cognac, 31
Howard Catherine, 37, 40
Howard, Thomas 3rd Duke of Norfolk,
36, 37, 44; Thomas 4th Duke of
Norfolk, 57
Huguenots, 2, 58, 59, 62, 70, 74, 98–99

Imperial election, 28
Intercursus Magnus, 5, 19
Intercursus Malus, 5, 20, 21
Ireland, 18, 19, 39, 68, 80, 99
Italy, 1, 7, 16, 17, 22, 23, 26, 31, 32, 33,
34, 50, 53, 54, 66, 83, 92; Florence, 5,
31; Milan, 1, 2, 27, 28, 31, 37;
Naples, 1, 2, 20, 92; Venice, 23, 31,
60; *see also* Papacy

James IV of Scotland, 18, 19, 24
James V of Scotland, 36, 40, 41
James VI of Scotland, 71, 72, 73–4
Joinville, Treaty of, 69
Jordan, W. K., 48, 49, 50

Le Havre, 45, 58, 59
Leicester, earl of, *see* Dudley, Robert
London, Treaty of, 25, 26, 28, 29, 30
Louis XII of France, 1, 16, 23, 24, 25,
27

Low Countries, *see* Netherlands and
Burgundy
Lübeck, 35
Lutherans or German protestants or
German princes, 32, 34, 35, 36–7, 44,
45

MacCaffrey, W. T., 13, 64
Mary I of England, 5, 8, 9, 12, 13, 28,
30, 31, 34, 50–5, 81, 82, 85, 92, 96, 98
Mary Stuart, Queen of Scots, 41, 43, 46,
48, 56, 57, 58, 66, 69, 71, 72, 73, 82,
93, 94, 99, 101
Maximilian I, Holy Roman Emperor,
16, 18, 19, 20, 21, 24, 27, 28, 89, 91
Medina del Campo, Treaty of, 15, 17,
18, 88
Merchant Adventures, 4, 6, 55, 70–1

navy, organisation of the, 9–10, 79
Netherlands, 2, 4–5, 9, 17, 18, 21, 34,
43, 47, 51, 55, 60–1, 62, 63–70, 74–6,
77, 78, 79, 83, 84, 98, 102–3, 104,
105–6; *see also* Burgundy
Nonsuch, Treaty of, 69
Norfolk, Duke of, *see* Howard, Thomas
Northumberland, *see* Dudley, John

Orange, William, Prince of, 61, 63, 64,
69, 74, 75

Pacification of Ghent, 66, 67, 68, 75
Paget William, 41, 49, 51, 52, 53, 54,
95–6
Palatinate, John Casimis of the, 67
Papacy, 21, 25, 31, 32, 33, 41, 44, 60,
68, 90; popes: Innocent VIII, 89;
Julius II, 23; Leo X, 24, 28, 30, 91;
Clement VII, 31, 32, 33, 34; Paul III,
35, Paul IV, 53, 54, 56
Parliament, 8, 11, 12–13, 19, 20, 27, 30,
33, 34, 50, 54, 89
Parma, *see* Farnese, Alexander
Philip II of Spain, 2, 5, 9, 13, 45, 50, 52,
53, 54, 55, 56, 60, 62, 64, 66, 68, 69,
74, 75, 76, 77–8, 85, 86, 96, 99, 100,
102, 104
Pinkie, battle of, 47
Pollard, A. F., 25, 39
Portugal, 5, 6, 10, 61, 68, 78, 79, 85

privateers, privateering, 4, 9, 10, 13, 14, 61, 63, 79, 85; *see also* Drake, Francis and Hawkins, John

Radcliffe, Thomas, Earl of Sussex, 2, 67, 72, 73, 74, 75, 82, 101, 102, 103–4
Rouen, 41, 79, 106

Sadler, Sir Ralph, 43, 93
Scarisbrick, J. J., 26, 40, 45
Scotland, 3, 8, 12, 15, 18, 19, 24, 27, 28, 35, 39, 40–4, 45, 46–8, 50, 54, 55, 56, 57–8, 71–4, 90, 95–6, 97
Sea Beggars, 63
Seymour, Edward, Earl of Hertford, Duke of Somerset, 38, 39, 43, 44, 45, 46–9, 94, 95
Shrewsbury, Earl of, *see* Talbot, Francis
Solway Moss, battle of, 41
Somerset, Duke of, *see* Seymour Thomas
Spanish ambassador, 68, 96; De Silva, 60; De Spes, 60, 62, 100; Renard, 52

Spurs, battle of, 24
Stafford, Thomas, 12, 53–4
Stuart, Esmé, 73
Sussex, Earl of, *see* Radcliffe, Thomas
Sweden, 5

Talbot, Francis, Earl of Shrewsbury, 54, 97
Tournai, 24, 25, 28
trade embargo, 4–5, 18, 60, 62, 89
Troyes, Peace of, 70
Turks, 6, 28, 34, 89

Walsingham, Sir Francis, 64, 67, 73, 74, 75, 76, 102–3
Warbeck, Perkin, 4, 17–20
Wernham, R. B., 30, 40, 41, 54, 63, 68, 82–3
Wilson, C, 63, 64
Winter, William, Admiral, 54, 57
Wolsey, Thomas, 25–30, 90–1
Wyatt, Thomas, 52, 53